For a
Culture
of **Life**

Konrad Raiser

For a
Culture
of Life

Transforming
Globalization
and Violence

Risk
BOOK SERIES

WCC Publications, Geneva

Cover design: Rob Lucas

ISBN 2-8254-1364-X

© 2002, WCC Publications, World Council of Churches
150 route de Ferney, P.O. Box 2100
1211 Geneva 2, Switzerland

No. 99 in the Risk Book Series

Printed in Switzerland

Contents

INTRODUCTION   vii

I. Transforming Globalization

1. GLOBALIZATION: THE CONCEPT AND ITS MEANING   3

2. HISTORICAL ROOTS OF GLOBALIZATION   8

3. GLOBAL CAPITALISM: A CRITICAL ASSESSMENT   14

4. DEMOCRATIZING THE INTERNATIONAL ORDER   28

5. CAN RELIGION "CIVILIZE" GLOBALIZATION?   40

6. THE ECUMENICAL VISION: AN ALTERNATIVE?   49

II. Towards a Culture of Reconciliation and Peace

1. RECONSIDERING PEACE AND JUSTICE   75

2. OVERCOMING VIOLENCE   83

3. IS THE "CLASH OF CIVILIZATIONS" UNAVOIDABLE?   99

4. HUMAN RIGHTS: FOUNDATION FOR A CULTURE OF PEACE   107

5. RECONCILIATION: A CHALLENGE TO THE CHURCHES   120

III. Moral and Spiritual Formation for a Culture of Life

1. TRANSFORMING GLOBALIZATION AND VIOLENCE   141

2. MORAL AND SPIRITUAL FORMATION   148

3. THE VISION OF THE OIKOUMENE   160

Notes   169

Introduction

Responding to globalization and overcoming violence are two focal points in the present activities of the World Council of Churches (WCC). They each have implications for the four overarching themes identified by the WCC central committee in 1999 on the basis of the guidelines for future activities decided by the Harare assembly. Being inter-related, they are intended to give coherence to the work of the Council. The four themes are: (1) being church; (2) caring for life; (3) witness and service amidst globalization; and (4) ministry of reconciliation. In preparation for the Harare assembly, I published a small book under the title *To Be the Church* which, unintentionally, anticipated one of those four areas. This book, even though not intentionally produced with this in mind, offers a contribution to the other three themes. The motif of sustaining and caring for life, the search for a "culture of life", has been running through most of the recent efforts to re-articulate the ecumenical vision in this age of globalization.

The three parts of this book draw on reflections originally presented in my reports as general secretary to the assembly and to the central committee since 1997, as well as in lectures and articles written for various occasions. I have also included material from earlier published writings and have indicated this in footnotes. Part I, though based on earlier written or spoken contributions to the discussion on globalization, has been written specifically for this publication. Part II includes substantial material from earlier writings, most of them originally published in German. Part III takes up again and develops further earlier reflections about the ecumenical vision; in its present form, it was written for this book.

I express my gratitude to the officers of the WCC and to my colleagues in the Staff Leadership Group of the Council for granting me the privilege of a short study leave to write this book. As a sign of appreciation, I dedicate it to them. None of us could foresee that the period of study leave and writing would coincide with the critical weeks after the tragic events in the United States of America on 11 September 2001. Unavoidably, I was drawn into the efforts to articulate an ecumenical response on behalf of the WCC to this situation. I have refrained from including here direct comment on the threat of terrorism and the question to what extent the process of globalization contributes to this new manifestation of conflict at global level. However, in treating together the challenges of globalization and violence, this book also addresses many of the issues arising as together we seek to discern how best to respond to such crises.

My hesitation to turn this book into a direct commentary on the brutal acts of terrorism on 11 September and on the political and military developments since then is rooted in the conviction expressed in the letter of 21 September 2001 to member churches in the United States: "This is indeed a time for quiet discernment of the 'signs of the time', for courage and wisdom, and to pray for God's guidance. As the prophet Isaiah says: 'In quietness and trust shall be your strength' (Isa. 30:15)." Moral, spiritual and political discernment needs time and space. The concluding chapter of this book discusses how the World Council of Churches is trying to provide a space for considering not only immediate responses, but also the root causes and long-term implications of the present crisis. This effort of critical assessment and of mutual consultation within the fellowship of the WCC is underway as this volume is being published.

In the second part, I recall and restate many of the fundamental convictions and affirmations which have guided the World Council in its response to the many conflicts over the last decade. These have served as the basis for the open letters written to member churches in the United States, to the secretary general of the United Nations and to leaders of the Muslim community. The WCC has consistently warned against the danger of returning to the logic of war in international relations, has appealed for the use of peaceful political means for resolving conflicts and has underlined the crucial role of the United Nations as the only legitimate framework for collective action to maintain international peace and security. However, as the discussion here on "humanitarian intervention" shows, complex ethical, political and juridical dilemmas arise in any attempt to respond to contemporary threats to peace and security. There are no easy answers, and thus the collective effort to discern the way forward is even more important.

Among these complexities is the fact that religious sentiments and loyalties are an element in many of the recent conflicts, including those around the terrorist attacks on 11 September. This is a fact that requires new serious reflection. Globalization has begun to transform the religious realm in ways which hitherto have not been sufficiently reflected in the context of inter-religious encounter. In my open letter to leaders of the Muslim community worldwide, published on 16 November 2001 on the occasion of the beginning of the month of Ramadan, I affirmed the relationship of trust and solidarity which has grown up over several decades of Christian-Muslim dialogue under the auspices of the WCC. Recent events make it necessary to find new ways to address together the pressing issues arising in a world rife with conflicts dividing Muslims and Christians.

The terrorist attacks on the World Trade Center and on the Pentagon seem to have been deliberately aimed at targets that symbolize the power and the global reach of the United States of America. Some analysts have suggested that they signify a fundamental shift to a militant and even violent rejection of the leading symbols of the forces shaping global culture. Religions, Christianity included, are based essentially on symbolic power. Discerning the "signs of the time" will therefore have to include a serious and self-critical attempt to discern how it is that religions whose teachings proclaim "peace", "shalom", "salaam", have been so readily co-opted to justify violence and war.

It is my hope that this book may contribute to this process of global discernment. It is a long process that will need to continue for many years to come.

KONRAD RAISER
November 2001

I
Transforming
Globalization

1. Globalization: The Concept and Its Meaning

Any attempt to come to terms with the contemporary world situation and the challenges it presents to the ecumenical movement will have to deal with the phenomenon of *globalization*. This is one of those terms that emerge in international discourse and serve to crystallize the perception of diverse trends, developments and features. The concept was first used some forty years ago and seems to be linked to the rapid changes in the field of mass communication, transforming the world into a "global village" (McLuhan). More specifically, the concept has come into use to describe developments in the world economy over the past ten years following the collapse of the communist empire in Eastern Europe.

Scores of books have been written since then, offering analyses and interpretations of the process of globalization. However, this has not necessarily brought more clarity. As has happened before with such fashionable concepts, globalization is used to cover such a range of features in the contemporary situation that the concept is beginning to lose its specific focus and thus its value as an analytical tool for interpretation. Some would therefore want to ban the concept altogether, at least from academic discourse, because in their view it has become so much linked with particular interests that it can no longer be used for analytical purposes.

Nevertheless it is possible to operate with a "working definition" and to point to a general set of features which tend to be subsumed under the term of globalization: i.e. the increase and intensification of interactions across state borders that involve all states and societies in a complex system of mutual interdependence, changing profoundly the role of states and non-state actors as well as the traditional patterns of social and cultural life. In the area of political action, this growing interdependence has been referred to as "internationalism" since the beginning of the 20th century. In the economic field, the same phenomenon has been covered by speaking of multinational or, more recently, transnational, corporations and business activities across state borders. In all these cases, the basic point of reference is the existence of nation-states as relatively self-contained and autonomous units entering into increasing relationships and interaction with each other.

Globalization marks a qualitative difference and advance in the character and intensity of this interdependence. It would appear that this change is related to the technological revolution in the field of electronics, often referred to as the "third industrial revolution", and its impact on information processing, communication, the mass media, transportation and production. The ability to store and process information with the help of computers and to transfer it instantaneously over any distance by telephone lines has given shape to the qualitatively new features of globalization. The PC, satellite communication and the Internet have become the symbols of this new reality, which has begun to supersede the traditional system of nation-states and their political and economic relationships.

The developments in information technology have been so fast and they are still continuing with the constant miniaturization of computer chips that we cannot yet assess with any degree of certainty the long-term implications of this revolution on human cultures and the ways of ordering political, social and economic life. There is, however, one area in which the advances in information technology and the means of electronic communication have brought about a qualitative change, i.e. the market of worldwide financial transactions. Whereas in 1973 daily foreign exchange trading amounted to US$10-20 billion, in 1996 the daily turnover was estimated to be over US$1.2 trillion, and it has now reached the level of $1.5 trillion, thus exceeding the total amount of foreign currency reserves of all the world's central banks. This explosion of the global capital market which has become the central driving force in the development of global capitalism has been possible only thanks to the advanced forms of information and communication technology. In their interaction these two factors determine the profile of contemporary globalization.

The electronic revolution, however, is beginning to affect the human condition far beyond its economic and financial applications. As Robert Schreiter has pointed out, the compression of space and time, the loss of the sense of distance and the creation of seeming simultaneity of events is changing the attachment of people to a particular territory and creates a sense of immediate neighbourhood, irrespective of distance. Time, as Schreiter says, "becomes a present with an edge of future reminding us of the constant obsolescence of the past".[1] The world is being experienced as a field of forces in constant movement without direction or a firm point of reference. Not only do national and territorial boundaries lose their significance, but also our understanding of history based on the linear conception of time is being shattered.

The weakening of territorial and historical differences and the interpenetration of cultural and social patterns due to the mobility of people and ideas as well as through advanced communication by way of the Internet places people as individuals and communities in a situation where they can no longer rely on inherited comprehensive cultural traditions. In fact, more and more, several cultures and religions occupy the same space and people can develop multiple identities. Shaping one's culture in order to affirm identity and mark a difference becomes a constant challenge in a world with fewer and fewer firm points of reference. If analyzed from this perspective, the emerging homogenized global culture is being unmasked as having the same virtual reality as the speculative financial transactions that have no reference to the real economy of production, trade and consumption.

However, the effective application of the new instruments of information technology and communication in the area of worldwide economic and financial transactions has become the dominant feature in the discussion about globalization. It provokes increasingly militant anti-globalization movements. Such protests against globalization focus particularly on the tendency among some of the promoters of global capitalism to present economic globalization as an inescapable result of the development of human society and to reject the possibility of any alternative.

This is the origin of much of the confusion that exists in the discussion about globalization. We need to deepen and advance the effort to analyze and interpret the process of globalization. It is therefore decisively important to make a distinction. On the one hand, there is the fact that worldwide interdependence has reached a qualitatively new stage through the technological revolution in the field of information processing and communication. On the other hand, there is the application of these instruments to different fields of human interaction. The Copenhagen Seminars for Social Progress, building on the results of the UN Summit Conference on Social Development in Copenhagen in 1995, propose that we distinguish between globalization

> as a stage in the historical evolution of humanity, and globalization as a political project steering the world economy in a particular direction. Calling the first a "trend" is to state that the narrowing of physical distances between peoples and the growing interdependence of countries represents both an unstoppable course of history, moved essentially by the application of human reason to the development of science and technology, and a general direction of change that can be navigated by human decision. The "project" is global capitalism, or the application of the ideas and institutions of the market economy to the world as a whole... Globalization is not moved by an invisible and benevolent hand. It is shaped by powerful actors and influenced by a multitude of forces, not all operating in the economic realm.[2]

This logical distinction, while necessary, is difficult to maintain and to apply in practice. The French language offers the two terms of *mondialisation* and *globalisation* to designate the two facets referred to above. The process of historical evolution of human society is of course inescapably influenced by human choices. All major technological breakthroughs have developed from previous human decisions about particular ends and means and they call for subsequent decisions about their use and the management of their consequences for the benefit of human society. The situation today with regard to the global perspectives created through the electronic technological revolution is not basically different from the challenges presented by previous industrial revolutions. The shrinkage in space and time that the world has experienced as a consequence of the technological revolutions in transport, communication and information processing is a historical fact from which there is indeed no escape. We are still far from having understood the long-term implications of this new configuration for social, political, cultural and religious institutions and forms of life. But this historical fact of the technology-driven process of globalization has to be distinguished from the deliberate use of the new possibilities to promote a specific policy project in the sense of global capitalism. "The distinction... is necessary to create space for human thinking and human action."[3] The challenge that is set before us is to ensure that the process of globalization serves to improve the conditions of human life at all levels and everywhere. This is essentially a political challenge calling for the development of rules and institutions of global governance that help to "civilize" globalization and to orient it towards serving the common good. Beyond the political challenge lies the need to reformulate ethical norms and values as well as cultural and religious traditions in the light of the emerging global reality.

2. Historical Roots of Globalization

The emergence of globalization is a complex process with multiple historical roots. Globalization as interpreted here in the sense of a qualitative change in the nature of human interdependence worldwide is indeed a relatively recent phenomenon. This makes it plausible to distinguish globalization from previous expressions of internationalism as well as from multinational and transnational forms of economic interaction. In this perspective, globalization appears as the ultimate and yet deeply ambiguous result of the process of modernity which aimed at understanding and ordering the world and social life on the basis of scientific investigation and rational choice. Modernity is rooted in the assumption of a rationally ordered universe and is propelled by the belief that its ideals can be universally applied. Modernity held out the promise of a continuous progress of individual liberties and material prosperity. Globalization presupposes the earlier stages in the development of modernity, i.e. the establishment of nation-states and of a system of international relations; the recognition of individual autonomy over against community obligations; the distinction between law and morality, establishing the rule of law as a universally applicable principle for resolving conflict instead of submitting to a particular system of religiously sanctioned moral norms; the process of liberating economic activity from the framework of state controlled mercantilism, and the emergence of the "market" as a more rational way of organizing economic exchanges based on the pursuit of the enlightened self-interest of all participants. The universalizing thrust is implicit and deeply rooted in the project of modernity, and the establishment of a global network of instantaneous communication disregarding the traditional limits of space and time seemingly brings the project to completion. The ambiguity of this process becomes apparent when we realize that globalization, like all previous stages in the process of modernization, produces winners and losers. While extending the effects of modernity throughout the world, at the same time it excludes growing numbers of people and leads to the fragmentation of communities. Further, while the emergence of the modern system of nation-states and the development of principles of international relations have been essential stepping stones for the process of globalization, the present-day manifestations of economic globalization seem to erode the very basis of the system of international relations of sovereign states. In these and several other respects, to be considered later, globalization appears not only as the culmination of the project of modernity, but also as opening the way to what is now called "post-modernity".

These ambiguities are particularly obvious when we consider the application of the new means of global interaction to the economic and financial realm. There have of course been forms of trade across state borders since the emergence of great empires and civilizations many thousand years ago. The late middle ages saw the emergence of companies and alliances engaged in long-distance trade, like the confederation of cities in the Hanseatic League or the trading companies of the Fugger and Welser. This process was intensified with the voyages of Columbus, Vasco da Gama and others, exploring other continents and preparing the way for the *conquista* of Latin America and later on for European colonialism. In fact, people in the southern hemisphere often experience the impact of globalization on their lives as a form of continuing colonial domination. Particularly the second half of the 19th century saw the continued expansion of colonialism and of international trade, and historians point out that between 1870 and 1920 economic integration had reached the point that one could speak of a *world* market.

The features of this form of economic integration are vividly captured in the following description given by the British economist John Maynard Keynes:

> The inhabitant of London could order by telephone, sipping his morning tea in bed, the various products of the whole earth, in such quantity as he might see fit, and reasonably expect their early delivery upon his doorstep; he could at the same moment and by the same means adventure his wealth in the natural resources and new enterprises of any quarter of the world, and share, without exertion or even trouble, in their prospective

fruits and advantages; or he could decide to couple the security of his fortunes with the good faith of the town's people of any substantial municipality and any continent that fancy or information might recommend. He could secure forthwith, if he wished it, cheap and comfortable means of transit to any country or climate without passport or other formality.[4]

In fact, the rapid processes of industrialization in Europe and the United States after 1870, the advances in transportation (railways) and communication (telephone and telegraph) as well as the completion of the European colonial expansion after the Berlin conference of 1884 created a first manifestation of global economic integration. There was stability in terms of trade between the main economic actors, and capital could move freely based on the gold standard.

> The history of the world economy since the industrial revolution had been one of accelerating technological progress, of continuous but uneven economic growth, and of increasing "globalization", that is to say of an increasingly elaborate and intricate worldwide division of labour; an increasingly dense network of laws and exchanges that bound every part of the world economy to the global system.[5]

This first period of globalization entered into crisis when the rivalry between the European powers led to the first world war. It came to an abrupt end with the world economic crisis 1929-33, leading into the second world war which marked the end of the European colonial empires and the emergence of the bipolar antagonism between the two ideological, political, military and economic blocks. In response to the catastrophic ending of the first experience of economic globalization, the agreements reached at the Bretton Woods conference in 1944 were intended to provide stability for international economic and financial transactions. Bretton Woods established a system of fixed currency relationships, with the US dollar serving as the lead currency, supported itself by the substantial gold reserves of the United States. It further established the three institutions, the International Monetary Fund, the International Bank for Reconstruction and Development (World Bank) and the General Agreement on Tariffs and Trade (GATT), which became the decisive instruments in shaping the course of the global economy. These measures were successful in achieving an unprecedented period of growth in the industrialized countries in the thirty years following the second world war. In most industrialized countries, this growth was accompanied by deliberate policies aiming at socially responsible distribution and creating and maintaining employment opportunities. The hopes that with the process of de-colonization the benefits of welfare state policies could be transferred to the newly independent countries in the South proved to be unrealistic, and by the end of the first development decade, the inner contradictions in this approach to managing the global economy were becoming obvious.

The two main contributing factors were, first, the oversupply of US dollars on the international capital market as a consequence of the Vietnam war, pushing the US government in 1971 to de-link the dollar from the gold standard. This brought to an end the cornerstone of the Bretton Woods agreement and opened the period of fluctuating currency relationships. The second factor was the oil crisis of 1973, leading to a dramatic increase in energy prices and reinforcing the pressures on the capital markets. This is the background for the decisive shift which took place in economic policy orientation, turning away from welfare economics to the monetarist approach of the Chicago school, placing the main emphasis on the control of money supply by the central banks and the fight against inflation by way of increasing interest rates in order to maintain the value of capital. This shift became a normative policy orientation with the adoption of neo-liberal monetarist economic policies by the Thatcher government in Britain after 1979 and the US government under President Reagan after 1981. One of the immediate consequences was the development of dramatic problems of international indebtedness, which attracted international attention with the threat of insolvency of Mexico in 1982. All efforts to contain the mounting debt crisis of countries in the South with the policy instruments adopted by the international financial institutions have so far proved a failure. This will be analyzed further in the next section. The decisive breakthrough towards economic and financial globalization occurred with the collapse of the communist system after 1989.

In fact, the system of a centrally planned economy in the communist countries had been an alternative version of the modernist paradigm.

Instead of entrusting the economy to the rationality of the self-regulating market, it placed the emphasis on the rationality of central planning to ensure equality of distribution. The collapse of communism left the capitalist approach as the only alternative under modernist assumptions. In addition, it liberated the capitalist system from the need to maintain its claim to serve social justice in the form of a "social market economy". Politically it removed the last imperial structure that had survived the competitive race of the 20th century and thus opened the way to the extension of the system of global capitalism into Eastern Europe and all other areas which had been under communist influence, including China.

This survey of the specific historical roots of the forms of globalization which have developed in the last decades of the 20th century cannot be concluded without pointing to one further factor which influenced the emergence of a global consciousness and at the same time has begun to challenge the assumptions of limitless progress built into the modern paradigm of universal rationality and its application to science and technology. Just as the revolutionary theories of Galileo, Kepler and Copernicus on the constitution of the universe had prepared the way for the early voyages of exploration and for the modern rational understanding of science, so the first explorations into outer space in the early 1960s dramatically demonstrated the finite and fragile limits of the planet earth. Since the first UN conference on the environment in Stockholm in 1972 and the publication of the report to the Club of Rome on *Limits to Growth* (1973), awareness has been growing that the modern form of industrialized and technology-driven economic life endangers the delicate web of natural processes which form the vital foundation for sustainable human community. This concerns not only the limited supply of natural resources, in particular energy resources, but also the availability of clean air and water, of arable land and the sustainability of the processes of food production. Pollution of air, water and soil through industrial production and waste can no longer be contained within national borders. They require transnational and considered global responses as in the form of the Climate Change Convention, with immediate implications for the prospects of unlimited economic growth.

3. Global Capitalism: A Critical Assessment

As has emerged clearly from this brief historical survey, the impact of globalization is most tangible in the field of world economy and finance. International economic and financial activity has evolved and intensified over a long period. Rules and institutional arrangements, like the Bretton Woods agreement of 1944, have been accepted in order to improve the management of international economic and financial transactions in the common interest of all. These arrangements have indeed brought about periods of stability and growth, most notably during the decades following the second world war. However, their scope has essentially been limited to the Western industrialized countries. They have excluded the "second" and "third" worlds, i.e. the countries under communist rule as well as the countries of the southern hemisphere that are still emerging from the period of colonialism.

The decisive transformation towards a global economic and financial system began, as has been indicated, in the early 1970s and has been propelled towards completion after the historic changes in 1989-90. Much of contemporary discussion and critical debate about globalization focuses on its manifestations in the economic and financial field. In order to avoid the frequent and misleading confusion with the historic process of globalization, it would be more appropriate to speak of "global capitalism". The following observations offer some considerations for a critical assessment of global capitalism, its impact and inner contradictions. Since several competent and comprehensive analyses have been carried out in the course of ecumenical discussions over the last decades, the following presentation draws freely on these resources.[6]

1. At the core of the neo-liberal paradigm which has taken the place of the earlier conception of a "mixed economy" lies the conviction that the unrestricted market mechanism, leaving all participants free to pursue their self-interest and thus to compete with each other, is the best way to achieve economic benefits in a situation of scarce resources. It is guided

by the belief that the free market, under the guidance of an "invisible hand", will in the long run produce the "greatest happiness of the greatest number". The key objective is to liberate economic activity from government interference through legal and other forms of regulation and to entrust all economically relevant activity to the initiative of private enterprise. Liberalization, deregulation and privatization are the central policy planks of the paradigm of the "free market".

The report on the Copenhagen Seminars for Social Progress opens the discussion on the economics of global capitalism with the following statements of principle:

> Markets are social constructs. They are institutions that developed throughout history from the realization by individuals that exchanges of goods and services were necessary for survival and useful for prosperity. Markets are elements of the social fabric shaped by laws, regulations, and the ideas, attitudes and interests of the actors involved. They operate with a mix of trust and legal contracts that vary with ways of thinking and tradition... There are many different types of local, national, regional and global markets. A market in the town square brings together buyers and sellers of farm and other products. A financier or lawyer participates in the management of the oil market or the operation of the stock market... The "Market", as often evoked in contemporary parlance, is an expression with an ideological connotation. Of late, this "Market" has been out-fitted with "forces", "constraints", "imperatives", "necessities", "requirements", and even "laws". Such mix of reification and deification of the "Market" does not contribute to the quality of market economies.

> A market economy is more than a "Market". As a social arrangement rooted on private property and freedom of initiative for the production and distribution of goods and services, a market economy is a complex and constantly evolving system of institutions, regulations and patterns of behaviour, with many actors, including public authorities. Market economies are instruments to serve human needs... At this point of history, the market economy system offers the best possibilities for improved standards of living in a context of respect for the fundamental civil and political rights of individuals.

Market economies, again as other necessary institutions, can function well or less well, can be efficient or wasteful. They can be improved, be made more efficient, more democratic and more humane, through changes in the behaviour of the economic actors. The assessment of the quality and performance of the market economy depends on the perspective and criteria that one adopts. Here, the perspective is the well-being of people throughout the world, the harmony of social relations within and among communities, and the welfare of future generations, particularly with regard to the protection of the environment and the "sustainability" of patterns of production and consumption.[7]

To take a critical look at the market paradigm is therefore not a question of being against markets as mechanisms for regulating economic activity. It is rather directed against the universalizing tendency presenting "the free market" as the primary framework for human activity. In fact, there is a wide range of directly or indirectly economically relevant interactions and social relationships in everyday life which do not follow the competitive logic of markets in the sense of pursuing pure self-interest, but which are based on cooperation, mutual trust and even care. They are the indispensable "infrastructure" which enables markets to function properly. When these interactions are also subjected to the market logic, the result is social fragmentation and disintegration.

Further, the situation of a perfectly free and competitive market that presupposes equality of opportunity among all actors is a theoretical construct which almost never corresponds to social and economic reality. When this theoretical assumption is taken as the baseline for policy prescriptions, it becomes the source of fundamental distortions. Through the short-term pursuit of self-interest, it deepens inequalities and produces long-term negative consequences for society. Therefore, it has always been acknowledged in the discussion about a market economy that public institutions and legal regulations are necessary to ensure the proper functioning of markets, to determine their limits and to protect society and its weaker members from the effects of an unrestricted market dynamic.

Markets therefore are important and powerful mechanisms which can and do produce beneficial results for society. However, their usefulness is limited, and when they are universally extended to cover all forms of social and economic activity they become destructive. Having invented the market mechanism, human society is faced with the need, on the local, national and global levels, to restrain the power of markets in the common interest.

In fact, the global extension of the neo-liberal market paradigm to all parts of the world and to all spheres of social and economic life has led to a concentration of power in fewer and fewer hands, escaping the democratic processes of legitimizing and controlling the exercise of power. Therefore, ecumenical discussion has led to the urgent call for an alternative paradigm, re-instating the character of economics as "political economy", recognizing the importance of historical, cultural and other contextual dimensions, shifting the focus from self-interest to common social concern for the well-being of all and for social sustainability, and recognizing the fundamental aspect of power in all human transactions.[8] Efforts to elaborate such an alternative paradigm, re-instating and developing further earlier forms of economic analysis prior to the introduction of the neo-liberal paradigm, have been underway for some time and are gaining influence even among mainstream economists.

2. The move towards global capitalism based on the neo-liberal paradigm began in the early 1980s. Reference has already been made to the deliberate change of economic policy in Great Britain and the United States. The radical change in Chile under the military government of Augusto Pinochet provided a initial testing ground. After the critical manifestation of the problem of international debt (Mexico), the international financial institutions adopted the basic principles of the new paradigm and developed their concept of "structural adjustment" with its central objective of stimulating economic growth in developing countries and thus enabling them to continue servicing their debts. To achieve this goal,

the national economies were to be opened up to the global market by stimulating exports; their competitiveness based on comparative advantages over against other economies had to be strengthened; and, most of all, they were to be persuaded or obliged to create conditions for attracting foreign investment.

The package of structural adjustment policies included some or most of the following measures: abolishing subsidies, cutting budgets, above all in the fields of education, health and social security, privatizing public sector enterprises, reducing taxation on corporate profits, deregulating working hours and wage agreements, and reducing social costs. Originally formulated with a view to developing countries, these measures have meanwhile also become part of a generalized framework of economic austerity policies in industrialized countries. They form a single standardized model – the so-called "Washington consensus" – for which the French discussion has coined the expression *la pensée unique*, and which is being applied without taking the particularities of specific countries into account.

The critical assessment of the impact of this move towards global capitalism should not fall into the ideological trap of adopting a position rejecting trade liberalization, growth or "the market" altogether. In a world with continuous population growth, comparable economic growth is necessary to secure employment, income and a decent standard of living for all people. The question rather is who benefits from this economic growth. There is no question either that open markets are more effective in engendering growth than centrally planned economies; the problem is rather one of access to the market, participation and the control of power. Finally, liberalizing trade and removing trade barriers and protectionism is in principle in the common interest of all countries; the difficulty arises with grossly unequal terms of trade.

If measured by their stated objectives, the results of the policies promoting global capitalism have to be judged critically – in spite of the limited success of the so-called "threshold countries" which have experienced high rates of growth and have been able to become active participants in the global economy, especially the "small dragons" in Asia, i.e. Korea, Malaysia, Singapore, Taiwan and Hong Kong. After having followed their single-minded policy directions for the last twenty years, even the leaders of the IMF and the World Bank now admit that "something is wrong... With all the forces making the world smaller, it is time to change our way of thinking... Growth is not enough. We must confront deeper-seated inequalities."[9]

The most obvious manifestation of the inherent contradictions in the system of global capitalism has been the way in which the dramatic increase of international indebtedness, especially of developing countries, has been handled. All responses up to the second, enhanced initiative for the highly indebted poor countries (Hipic II) have been formulated from the perspective of the creditors (private banks, governments, international financial institutions) in the interest of maintaining the viability of the system. They have been based on the application of the rigid orthodoxy of the Washington consensus as defended by the IMF, irrespective of the consequences for the populations of indebted countries and their living conditions. Most recently, the dramatic results of this approach have become visible in Argentina, which had faithfully followed and implemented all directives from the IMF, leading to the total impoverishment of the population of a country which used to pride itself in belonging to the rich and developed part of the world. Indeed, something is fundamentally wrong with a system that does not allow the abolition of the state of debt bondage that is crippling the prospects of recovery for a growing number of countries and even whole regions.

Gross inequalities and a dramatically widening gap between rich and poor, both between industrialized and developing countries as well as within most countries, is in fact the most obvious critical result of twenty years of global capitalism. In particular, the difference in income between the wealthy 20 percent living in the industrialized countries and the poorest 20 percent has increased from a ratio of 30:1 in 1960 to the proportions of 70:1 in the year 2000, i.e. it has more than doubled in spite of several development decades and twenty years of growth-oriented policies. The richest 20 percent today receive 86 percent of the global income, whereas the poorest 20 percent have to be content with a mere 1.2 percent.

Another way of presenting this dramatic inequality is to state that 1.2 billion people today live on an income of less than 1 US dollar per day and 2.8 billion still have less than 2 US dollars per day. In spite of deliberate policies to liberalize trade and financial flows, more than 80 percent of world trade and direct foreign investment has remained within the "triad countries" formed by the European Union, the United States and the countries of Northeast Asia. The result has been a massive strengthening of the power of transnational corporations which control a large part of world trade, investments and the development of new technologies. In fact, the policy emphases on liberalization, deregulation and privatization have been promoted actively by corporate interests and have been the main means of strengthening their global power. In addition, global competition has led to a wave of corporate mergers, reducing constantly the number of competitors and creating business empires whose financial power surpasses that of middle-sized national economies.

The impact of these policies has been particularly dramatic for the countries of Central and Eastern Europe who have been exposed to the full force of global capitalism since 1989. While acknowledging that there are significant differences between the countries concerned, a UNDP survey of 1999 came to the conclusion that during a period of only ten years, the level of poverty rose tenfold, while at the same time a small group of "winners" had been able to amass excessive levels of wealth. In some of the countries, life expectancy had fallen significantly; health care, schooling and educational standards had declined, and overall commerce-related criminal activity had increased dramatically.

Four further consequences need to be mentioned, at least briefly. The first concerns the question of food security in the countries of the global South. The pressure to integrate their economies into a grossly unequal world market has eroded the capacity of many countries to provide for the basic food requirements of their own populations and increased their dependency on transnational agro-business. The second is the impact in the area of employment. From the perspective of corporate interests, labour represents a cost factor that must be reduced in order to increase competitiveness and profitability. Much of the economic growth in recent decades in the North as well as the South is "jobless" growth, leaving behind a massive problem of structural unemployment and pushing more and more people into the informal economy. Thirdly, global capitalism and the dominant position of transnational corporations have dramatically affected world trade. In particular the terms of trade for goods that are of vital importance for developing countries have suffered from forced trade liberalization. Finally, the policies of global capitalism have aggravated the threat to ecological sustainability in the form of deforestation, soil erosion and desertification, the dumping of polluted and poisonous industrial waste, the rapid reduction of bio-diversity and the continued process of global warming, with the attendant danger of dramatic climate changes.

3. As has been indicated before, the dynamic of global capitalism has drawn much of its energy from the progressive liberalization and deregulation of the financial market. It is estimated that today global financial transactions amount to US$1.5 trillion every day. Only 5 percent of this enormous volume is related to trade in goods and services or to productive investment. The vast majority represents "virtual", speculative transactions seeking to profit from changing currency exchange rates and interest rates, as well as banking on anticipated changes in the values of equities. All of this has been facilitated by the development of a global information and communication network.

The fragility of this global financial market has been demonstrated by the Asian financial crisis of 1997, which was only the last and most dramatic of a long series of crises since 1982. These crises have had immediate effects on the internal economic and financial situation in developing countries, including Asia, as the examples of Thailand, Indonesia and the Philippines show. The industrialized countries enjoy slightly better protection because of their larger markets.

Investors are looking for secure placements for their capital and try to evade political restrictions, e.g. through taxation, as much as possible. This has led to the multiplication of so-called offshore financial centres and tax havens, to widespread practices of money laundering, especially of funds derived from narco-traffic and arms deals, as well as to capital flight from developing countries. It is estimated that developing countries in this way are losing annually some US$ 50 billion, which is roughly equivalent to the total annual flow of aid to these countries and represents six times the cost of achieving universal primary education or almost three times the cost of providing universal primary health care.

Some countries, like Chile, Malaysia, China and Russia, have re-introduced certain forms of capital control in order to prevent or at least slow down the movement of speculative capital. At the same time, the volatility of the deregulated financial market has led to the establishment of a series of coordinating mechanisms in connection with the Bank of International Settlements in Basle with the aim of promoting more financial stability. However, all these arrangements have so far benefited only the more powerful economies, leaving the developing countries on their own. All more far-reaching proposals and demands for a fundamental reshaping of the architecture of the global financial system, including the role of the international financial institutions, have so far met with the determined resistance of the US government and of the powerful corporate lobbies.

4. Such proposals for changes in policy and institutional arrangements have been advanced by the United Nations

Development Programme since 1992.[10] They aim at the establishment of effective forms of global governance, a concern to which we will return in the next section. More specifically with regard to the global economic and financial system, most proposals agree that the present institutions of the IMF, the Bank of International Settlements and other more recent arrangements should be replaced by something like a world financial authority. Such an authority would have the mandate to manage global financial markets, to establish rules for capital transfers, to enforce common levels of taxation, especially for transnational business activities, and to exercise oversight and regulation of commercial banking, securities and insurance business. There is also a proposal to set up an independent arbitration-mechanism for international debts and an orderly procedure for handling cases of state insolvency or bankruptcy as a consequence of unmanageable debt, following the model of legal provisions in the national economies of most industrialized countries. There is also a call for the establishment of an international convention for the repatriation of illegally acquired capital. The most widely discussed proposal is the introduction of a currency transaction tax, suggested as early as 1978 by the Nobel Prize-winning economist James Tobin, the so-called "Tobin tax". Even a marginal taxation in the order of 0.1 percent, which could subsequently be increased, would serve to curb speculative financial trading and could generate up to US$200 billion in annual revenues to be used for genuine purposes of social development.

Other proposals suggest a restructuring of all development-oriented instruments and programmes of the United Nations, combining the present mandates of the World Bank, the World Trade Organization, the United Nations Trade and Development Organization, and other instruments under a strengthened Economic and Social Council, which might become an effective counterpart to the existing UN Security Council. Recognizing the increasing importance of non-governmental organizations in the field of social development, provision should be made for their effective participation in formulating and implementing global policies in the field of social and economic development. The secretary general of the United Nations is promoting a "global compact" with the aim of combining the power of the existing international financial institutions and of transnational corporations in a voluntary effort to adopt basic objectives of social development, in particular the reduction of world poverty by 50 percent by the year 2015. This cannot, however, be regarded as a satisfactory response to the need for more effective participation by the global networks of nongovernmental organizations.

New institutional arrangements for global policy formation are especially needed with regard to the challenges of ecological sustainability. The 1992 UN Conference on Environment and Development at Rio with its decisions on climate change, bio-diversity and the agenda 21 called for an effective framework for implementation nationally and internationally. However, the UN Commission on Sustainable Development and the UN Environment Programme have not been given either the resources or the authority to respond to this challenge. The forthcoming World Summit on Sustainable Development in 2002 will make evident the failure of the international community to act on the agenda formulated ten years ago at Rio. In particular, the negotiations regarding the Kyoto Protocol on Climate Change reveal that the policy orientation towards "sustainable development" is serving more the interests of global capitalism than furthering "sustainable communities" and ecological justice.

Particular critical attention is being directed at the most recent part of the global architecture, the World Trade Organization, which in 1995 took the place of the former GATT. Since the failure of the WTO ministerial meeting in 1999 in Seattle, this criticism has become a matter of public discussion. While the WTO, in contrast to the limited representativeness of the other international financial institutions, is built on the democratic consensus principle of all member countries, its promotion of the liberalization of trade has not resulted in the expected large gains for developing countries. Rather, it has increased inequalities and has been unable to reverse the deterioration of the terms of trade. The procedures for decision-making in the WTO are highly secretive, discriminate against the weaker member states and lack public accountability. The decision of the recent ministerial conference of the WTO at Doha to open a new round of negotiations for liberalization in the areas of agriculture, services, investments and intellectual property rights has failed to redress the negative effects of existing agreements and tackle the inequalities in the trade arena which are among the most significant obstacles to genuine social development.

A UNDP study of 1999 on *Global Public Goods*[11] is a fundamental conceptual challenge to the present international policy agenda with its focus on liberalization, deregulation and privatization. It addresses those negative consequences of the present practices of global capitalism that are regarded as *externalities* in orthodox market theory. So far national and international policy agendas limit themselves to reducing these negative effects rather than addressing the root causes. These *externalities* have to be considered as examples of market failure calling for the formulation of a global public policy agenda directed towards the provision of those goods which need to be secured at global level. The study distinguishes between three main classes of global public goods. The first includes *natural global commons*, such as the ozone layer or climate stability, where the policy challenge is sustainability, and the collective action problem is one of over-use. In the second class are *human-made global commons* which "encompass a range of diverse issues: scientific and practical knowledge, principles and norms, the world's common cultural heritage and transnational infrastructures such as the Internet. For these global public goods, the main challenge is under-use." Finally the study mentions *global policy outcomes,* which include "peace, health and financial stability. The collective action problem associated with these less tangible global public goods is the typical challenge of under-supply."[12] The detailed analysis of this study leads to far-reaching consequences for creating new international institutional structures.

Ultimately, however, what is needed to redress the negative impact of the policies promoting global capitalism is not only a reshaping of institutional structures but a radical review of the underlying neo-liberal economic policies. A study prepared by the "Ecumenical Coalition for Economic Justice" with a view to the United Nations Conference on Financing for Development in 2002 formulates the demand for an alternative development model in the following terms: "Experience over the past two decades shows that these policies [i.e. those promoted by the World Bank and in the International Monetary Fund] have failed to meet even their own goals of attracting investment to developing countries and fostering growth. Far from reducing poverty or enhancing ecological sustainability, these policies have widened the gap between the wealthy and the poor, and have resulted in greater social exclusion and greater exploitation of the earth's resources.

> For the ecumenical community, authentic human development can never be achieved when the ultimate goal is the amassing of wealth and material goods, creating an unquenchable thirst for more power, profits, and positions. An alternative approach is required that allows us to express "development" and "economy" in relation to our common vocation to live in right relationship with our neighbours, with the earth and with our creator. Such an approach includes these key affirmations:
>
> - A *recognition* that real value cannot be expressed in monetary terms and that life – and that which is essential to sustain it – cannot be commodified.
> - A *belief* in the inherent dignity of every person and a priority on creating the conditions for a dignified life.
> - A *commitment* to an economy whose role is to serve the well-being of people and the health of the earth.
> - A *focus* on the ultimate aim of economic life to nurture sustainable, just and participatory communities.
> - A *vision* of a global community whose interdependence is not reduced to trade and markets.

- An *acknowledgment* of a common destiny as co-inhabitants of the one earth for which we all share responsibility and from which we should all equally benefit.
- A *responsibility* to uphold the right of all people – particularly the diverse communities of the poor and excluded – to participate in the economic, social and political decisions which affect them.[13]

4. Democratizing the International Order

The process of globalization poses new challenges for the international order that has developed since the second world war. The centre-piece of this order is the United Nations Organization created in 1945 to secure world peace, and to promote the respect of human rights and a decent standard of living for people everywhere. Through its various specialized organizations and programmes, the UN has made a lasting contribution to the improvement of the livelihood of billions of people, especially in the southern hemisphere.

For decades, the UN was prevented from responding fully to its mandate owing to the antagonism of the two political, military and ideological power blocks. With the collapse of communism in Central and Eastern Europe and the end of the cold war, the United Nations has gained a new opportunity to establish its central role in shaping a viable world order. However, the forces of global capitalism and the dominant role of the United States have further weakened the influence of the United Nations. What is at stake is the transition from the traditional system of international relations to an order of truly global governance able to respond to the challenges of globalization.

1. It has become common parlance to speak of the "international community" with the implication that it should take certain actions, e.g. against those who threaten world peace and security or violate human rights. This presupposes the existence of a common framework of values, commitments and obligations, which binds peoples and states together. The charter of the United Nations could be considered as the founding document of this community, but we are still far from an agreed understanding of responsibilities and obligations that would turn such an association of states into an "international community".

The entire international system is based on the voluntary agreement of autonomous sovereign nation-states to cooperate with each other on the basis of contracts or treaties. International conventions or covenants negotiated under UN auspices are multilateral treaties, which become part of the complex system of international law once they have been ratified by a specifically defined number of national states. The United Nations has contributed significantly to the development of a normative international law, but its validity is based on the willingness of sovereign states to abide by these norms.

The classical notion of sovereignty includes the principles of the equality of rights of all states – irrespective of size, economic resources or political power; the inviolability of frontiers; and non-interference in internal affairs. Sovereignty is the counterpart on the collective level to human autonomy on the individual level. Sovereignty further implies that those exercising the power of government are accountable only to the citizens of their respective country or territory, even for actions on the international level. This also means that for centuries war was considered a legitimate expression of state sovereignty. Only under the impact of two world wars have efforts to develop an international legal framework to regulate warfare begun to bear fruit.

This modern system of international relations based on the cooperation of sovereign nation-states represents a significant advance over the previous constellation of competitive empires. Its origin is the peace treaty of Westphalia in 1648 and it is based – at least in the Western world – on the separation of religion and politics, of law and morality. The conduct of public affairs is to be guided by reason, religious and ethnic tolerance, basic equality of rights of all citizens and the rule of law. Loyalty to the nation in exchange for the recognition of the status of citizen takes the place of the religious legitimization of imperial power. In its developed form of constitutional democracies, this modern pattern of nation-states has been extended to all parts of the world and is considered to be the most rational and effective system of governance, providing for a balanced relationship of freedom and order.

2. It has been the assumption that the issues of international order would find their solution once all states were governed

in this democratic way. However, the very defence of sovereignty and national self-interest allows the system of nation-states again and again to be dominated by geopolitical factors where the balance of power between powerful states becomes the over-riding concern. The Security Council of the United Nations, with veto power given to the five permanent members, reflects this situation. In any case, the international system based on the relationship of sovereign nation-states does not yet meet the demands of democratic governance.

The weakness and fragility of this system began to become apparent when the first challenges of a truly global nature appeared: e.g. the threat of nuclear warfare, the danger of the disintegration of the ecosystem, or at least of vital parts of it, and the problems created by worldwide movements of migrants and refugees. The system lacks appropriate mechanisms to reconcile the self-interest of nation-states, in particular of the powerful ones, with the common interest of the survival of the human community as a whole. The international human-rights instruments have so far failed to provide the system with a common foundation.

The process of globalization has sharpened this challenge considerably. The shrinkage of space and time is beginning to undermine the significance of territorial boundaries and of national identity based on a common history. Migration puts the modern notion of citizenship based on nationality under pressure. The free flow of capital, but also of drugs and arms, creates conditions which are beyond the reach of national governments. The agreements on trade in commodities and services within the framework of the World Trade Organization have further limited the power of national policy making. New actors, in the form of transnational corporations and the interlinked networks of civil society, have emerged. They make effective use of the means of globalization and begin to influence the formulation of international policy. In addition, the technological rationality of globalization seems to favour an understanding of global reality in terms of self-regulating systems which no longer need political intervention.

Meanwhile this process of weakening of the international system has been aggravated further through the spread of the neo-liberal ideology as the basis for policy-making on national as well as international levels. In the neo-liberal perspective, the role of the state has to be limited to creating the conditions for the free play of market forces, which is considered to be the most rational and effective way of satisfying human needs. In the interest of maintaining competitiveness in the global market, public concerns for the common good are downgraded, and the role of government is reduced to economic and financial management, whereas actual power has been transferred to the principal "global players".

In many ways this transformation of the political order, both nationally and internationally, is a logical consequence of the modern focus on instrumental rationality and its universalizing tendency, disregarding historical, social and cultural differences. The hitherto dominant expression of a modern society in terms of a constitutionally governed democracy granting rights to its citizens and serving the common good is progressively being replaced by a "market society", where citizens are being reduced to consumers and competition becomes the ultimate means for resolving conflicts of interest.

It is the irony of the present process of globalization under the influence of global capitalism that this transformation of the political order has been and is being promoted actively by democratically elected governments. The weakening of the authority of the state and, by implication, of the international system is not an unavoidable consequence of globalization: it is rather part of a particular political project. What emerges is a thoroughly non-democratic order without legitimacy, equal participation or accountability. However, even the "global players" need the states since it is they who remain "the only political form that exerts authority in a way that is fully acknowledged on the global level".[14] The challenge therefore is to reshape the notion of sovereignty and to redefine the role of states in the enlarged global context.

The process of constructing the European Union is an important testing ground in this regard.

3. The process of globalization calls for a determined effort to re-imagine a political order, both nationally and internationally, which can respond to the new reality. It seems, however, that the dominance of the neo-liberal economic ideology has destroyed the capacity for political imagination. The discrediting of the socialist alternative and the virtual silencing of what used to be the non-aligned movement has left the global field to pure power politics driven by economic and financial interests. Many people respond to this situation with a sense of fatalism. They are disillusioned with regard to the problem-solving capacity of those in positions of public leadership. They have lost trust and confidence in the political process because of the obvious lack of transparency, accountability and opportunities for participation in decision-making. They regard the transfer of power to the corporate level as an inevitable consequence of globalization and they therefore increasingly abstain from participation even in democratic elections, thus further weakening the basis of legitimacy and authority of governments.

Others accept the "social Darwinism" of the neo-liberal ideology as the ground rule for politics as well and return to an authoritarian understanding of public order. When the political process degenerates into a zero sum game in which there are only winners and losers in the struggle to accumulate power and wealth, the notion of the common good becomes ineffective and societies begin to disintegrate. It is against this background that we need to understand the resurgence of the various forms of ethno-nationalism. Where the coherence of nation-states providing a common identity to their citizens is being undermined we see the emergence of militant or even violent forms of identity politics re-establishing and defending an exclusive form of collective identity to counteract the fragmentation resulting from economic globalization.

Historic memory could point to the fact that the present situation is not dissimilar to that of the late 19th and the first part of the 20th century when liberal capitalism first appeared on the scene. Its negative consequences in terms of growing inequalities, unemployment and social dislocation were countered by the struggle of the international labour movement and were finally redressed through the introduction of welfare politics. Many of the contemporary efforts to find an effective political response to globalization try to revive the economic and political principles that helped to re-stabilize the political order after the second world war. However, such attempts seldom transcend the dominant mentality of functional rationality. At best they arrive at procedural and institutional proposals for improving the management of public affairs nationally and internationally, and achieving a better balance of conflicting power interests. They do not provide a vision for "humane global governance".[15]

One of the reasons for this obvious lack of political imagination is the fact that the modern understanding of politics has tended to relegate the question of common values defining the desired shape of society to the realm of individual choice and preference. Most societies have been held together by an inheritance of traditional common values often with secularized religious roots. Democracies cannot function without such a foundation of shared values. However, it is one of the effects of globalization that this base, which has been taken for granted, is now beginning to disintegrate. It would therefore be important for politics to involve itself in a debate about those values that could provide the foundation for a new political order and to create the political space where competing values and rights can engage with each other in a common search. Yet, "in secularized and liberal societies attaching prime importance to the freedom and rights of the individual, to probe into the philosophical foundations of the common perception of what constitutes a good life and a good society is often seen as futile".[16]

One way in which this "abstentianism" expresses itself is the distinction between "serious" and "soft" values. Concern for social justice, solidarity, care, compassion and generosity is considered "soft" over against the dominant values of competitiveness, efficiency, individual autonomy and acquisition of money and power. The Copenhagen Seminars for Social Progress come to this conclusion:

> The current hierarchy of soft and serious values is at the root of the conception of economic rationality and at the origin of the marginalization of "social" concerns. The "social" is "soft". It is understood as what is relevant for the people who are not in power. It is a "problem" or a mere "consequence" of economic decisions... The building of a global democratic community requires profound changes in this dominant ethos and a revisiting of the distinction between "soft" and "hard", "core" and "subordinate" values and policies.

Recognizing that an ethos of solidarity, care and compassion is an integral part of the religious heritage of humankind, many participants in this discussion call for a new culture which can overcome the secular separation of religion and politics and incorporate the values rooted in religious traditions. In any case, while democracy is "secular" in the sense of allowing a plurality of views and beliefs, it should not be seen as hostile to religion or indifferent to morality and to the spiritual traditions of humanity.

4. The report on the Copenhagen seminars concludes with a chapter on a "humanist political culture", or a "call upon ideals and utopias". "It is time to rehabilitate ideals and utopias," in the sense of a critical stance against the established order. "After all, global capitalism is in fact a utopia – 'prosperity and happiness for all' – often disguised into a natural phase in the evolution of the world economy."

The report provides a number of criteria to which a new global political project would need to respond:
- It would "require a strong ethical basis, clear moral orientations, and an enriched vision of the direction and components of progress for humanity..."
- It would "have to be universal in its conception and ambition... Rejection of the globalization of many facets of

human activities and aspirations would be absurd and unwarranted..."
- It would "have to see development in its totality... The current view that public goods, apart from the military, are not part of an efficient economy, will have to be fundamentally revised...

Ultimately, the aim of a new global political project would be to establish a truly democratic structure of global governance. This means that democracy "has to be both reinvented and promoted. It has to be imagined internationally and globally, while being defended in local, national and regional settings." All too often democracy is being reduced to the exercise of individual liberty and the pursuit of self-interest at the expense of the fundamental requirements of equality and participation in public decision-making.

The chapter on the dimensions of a global democracy in the report of the Copenhagen seminars opens with the following "definition" of democracy:

> Democracy is a set of procedures and institutions through which citizens participate directly or indirectly in the elaboration and implementation of the laws that govern the community; it is also a regime protecting and promoting human rights; and it is a culture shaping individual and collective behaviour. Each of these dimensions is indispensable to the other.

Judged in the light of this description of a democratic order, it is obvious that the present political order, responding primarily to the logic of the market, cannot be considered as being democratic. "Global capitalism is not a democratic affair." In fact, the massive influence exercised by economic and financial interest groups on the political process erodes the very principle of participation. The same is true for the institutional frameworks within which the most important political decisions for the global community are being taken, i.e. the International Monetary Fund, the World Bank, the OECD and the G8 nations, as well as the boards of transnational corporations and international banking institutions.

It is true that democracy is a demanding form of political organization that continually has to be defended against failure and misuse. There is no uniform, normative model of democracy, and democratic principles of governance lead to different procedural and institutional arrangements at the different levels from the local to the global. However, the following principles must guide the search for a humane and democratic order. It must effectively prevent a centralization of power, defend the rule of law and allow for participation of citizens in decisions affecting them as well as the whole of society. It must strive to establish a transparent form of governance, holding those in authority publicly accountable and opening public space for critical debate, particularly through the public media.

5. The search for a new global political project has become one of the points of crystallization for the emergence of an international civil society. It is generally agreed that civil society includes the range of social movements working on issues of humanitarian concern, public welfare and human rights that are independent of government and of business. In recent years, the growth of civil society internationally which has taken place in parallel with the process of globalization has been seen as a strong democratic development. While 6000 international non-governmental organizations were registered in 1990, their number has now increased to 26,000. Several important political events or policy decisions are credited largely to successful campaigning by civil society organizations, e.g. the victory of the "people's power revolution" in the Philippines, the movement against impunity in Latin America, the international campaign to ban land mines, the Jubilee 2000 debt relief campaign and campaigns for the implementation of Agenda 21 following the Earth Summit in Rio de Janeiro in 1992.

The Copenhagen Seminars on Social Progress count social movements and non-governmental organizations as important social forces at international level, pursuing a genuinely global agenda. They distinguish three types of such organizations, i.e. those focusing on issues of social justice and human rights, often with a strong ethical and spiritual orientation; those lobbying for particular causes and responding to weaknesses in the official political process; and those with militant and exclusivist political, religious or ideological orientations rejecting the foundations of a democratic order. It is obvious that only the first two types can be considered as democratizing social forces and it should be noted that organizations whose main purpose is lobbying for particular projects are not "immune from various forms of political or financial corruption". Nevertheless, these movements and organizations are indispensable for shaping a new form of global governance. In fact, they have become so influential that there is some concern about their impact on the legitimacy of governmental and intergovernmental institutions. It is therefore imperative to find new forms of interaction between the levels of government, business and civil society if a new democratic culture is to emerge. In particular, civil society needs open spaces for public debate and negotiation. This, however, presupposes that social movements and organizations in civil society

> should guard their separate identities and avoid assuming direct governmental responsibilities. They also should avoid adopting the values of the market economy and copying the ethos of private companies, including profitability or competitiveness... If democratic societies are to be built on a "tripod" made of public institutions, market institutions and civil organizations – including the trade unions – then each component has to hold on to its separate identity and responsibilities.

Richard Falk has become one of the most articulate advocates of strengthening the active participation of social movements and organizations in civil society in the shaping of the global agenda. He has even advanced the vision of a "global people's assembly" in order to increase the legitimacy of the structures of global governance. It should be recalled that the preamble of the charter of the United Nations begins with the words "We, the peoples of the United Nations..." This is a reminder of the fact that democratic governance rests on legitimization by the people themselves. The system of state sovereignty needs to be complemented by the legitimacy and the power of popular sovereignty. The enlargement of the European institutions by establishing the European Parliament elected directly by the people of the member countries is taken as a model for creating a similar people's assembly at global level.[17]

In his response to the report of the Copenhagen Seminars on Social Progress, as well as in several of his other publications, Richard Falk takes this assessment of the significance of social movements and organizations in civil society for a democratic order and applies it to the task of transforming globalization. He introduces the distinction between "globalization from above", represented essentially by transnational business and international financial organizations, and "globalization from below", promoted by the networks of civil society or a "new internationalism". "It is my view that the predominant creative energy for compassionate globalization under present world conditions derives mainly, although not exclusively, from GFB (Globalization from Below)."[18]

Falk is convinced that this emerging global civil society will be successful in transforming globalization only if it develops a "politically engaged spirituality", i.e. acknowledges the religious and spiritual roots of its ethical ideals and enters into alliances with the world's religious communities. In this sense, the religious resurgence can have an important influence on the future shaping of global civil society. He summarizes his reflections in the following terms:

> The future of globalization is very uncertain and will assert itself unevenly in different parts of the world. Likewise, the responses to its burdens and benefits will be diverse. The role of religion as a way of either confronting globalization, as in its most extreme manifestations, or of "humanizing" globalization by the advocacy of a global ethic is likely to remain important for the foreseeable future. Religious activists are also likely to play an important part in resisting those implications of global-

ization that appear to produce suffering and distorted priorities, and thereby encourage various social forces to join together in building up global civil society along morally and spiritually sensitive lines. The prospects for creating some form of humane global governance in the 21st century seem likely to depend on whether the religious resurgence is able to provide the basis for a more socially and politically responsible form of globalization than what currently exists.[19]

5. Can Religion "Civilize" Globalization?

1. The impact of globalization on the religious field is ambiguous. In its most generalized form, globalization reinforces interdependence between peoples and societies, including their cultures and religions. Hitherto self-contained and more or less homogeneous cultural and religious spaces are being opened up, leading to increased interaction. As a consequence, truth claims are relativized and new religious movements emerge together with more fluid contours of religious identities. Globalization in this sense is a direct cause of the increase in the religious plurality that has begun to manifest itself in all parts of the world.

At the same time, globalization has spread the dominant features of Western secular modernity, with its emphasis on instrumental rationality, individual autonomy, material progress and privatization of religion, across the whole world. In particular the ubiquitous presence of the symbols of consumerism (McDonald, Coca Cola, blue jeans, etc.) creates the impression of a powerful push towards cultural uniformity, which would further marginalize religious traditions.

There is, however, a powerful side effect to the contrary. As has been discussed above, one of the central features of Western modernity has been the formation of secular nation-states as the basic form of public governance. The process of de-colonization led to the setting up of a large number of new nation-states, largely based on the borders drawn up by the colonial powers. Much effort has gone into nation-building and democratization, largely following Western models. However, the process of globalization under the impact of global capitalism and the conditions imposed by structural adjustment programmes have significantly weakened the authority and legitimacy of these structures of governance. This has brought to the fore the artificial character of the new nation-states which are not yet held together by a common civic identity. In a situation where more and more people are utterly disillusioned about the prospects associated with modernization and development and the capacity or willingness of the new political and economic elites to deliver on their promises, they feel abandoned and are thrown back on earlier ethnic, cultural or religious identities to provide a sense of coherence and purpose for their lives. Under the impact of globalization a rapid process of fragmentation on the political and social level has taken place, provoking in turn a reaffirmation of more localized, religiously based, collective identities. They can enter into competition for power, resources and influence, often resulting in violent conflicts. Political leaders, in turn, have begun to exploit religious sentiments so as to mobilize people in support of their claims to power. The disintegration of political entities like the former Yugoslavia, and the conflicts in Indonesia, Nigeria and many other African countries provide dramatic evidence of this.

2. It is in this context that an intensive and controversial discussion has developed around the observation that globalization seems to be accompanied by a "resurgence" of religion, not only in Asia and Africa, but equally in Western societies. It would therefore seem necessary to reassess the widely accepted thesis that secularization is an inevitable consequence of modernization.

Secularization is commonly understood as the process by which the public space claims autonomy from religious control. Politics, economy and culture are recognized as having their own intrinsic logic based on functional rationality. Religion is privatized as an expression of individual faith or belief. Secularization is not necessarily anti-religious and can live alongside an affirmation of religious liberty and a positive acknowledgment of religious plurality. However, the more common expectation has been that religion would progressively disappear from public life and that a modern secular society would be indifferent and neutral towards religion.

Against this background the revitalization of religious traditions and in particular the reappearance of religion in the public arena seems to call for a critical reassessment of the secularization thesis. While it is true that modernization has led to a privatization of religion, the ambiguous effects of globalization on human life in community apparently reawaken the potential of religion to deal with experiences of uncertainty and contingency and to provide a comprehensive sense of meaning and identity by reference to a transcendent reality. Globalization, on the one hand, reinforces and spreads the universalizing thrust of modernization; on the other hand, it seems to produce a "re-enchantment" of social and cultural life and a progressive process of "de-secularization" (Peter L. Berger). This is linked to the fact that religious symbols and practices are woven into the everyday life of people and thus can offer a sense of protection over against the "colonizing" effects of globalization.

What, from a Western perspective, appears as "de-secularization", in the form of the emergence of strongly politicized forms of Islam, Hinduism and Buddhism, is viewed differently in the eyes of the non-Western world. Here, neither the differentiation of religion and culture as distinct frameworks nor the secular separation of religion and politics has taken root. In fact, many of the new nation-states, particularly in Asia, are based on an arrangement with the influential religious communities. The "secular" constitutions of India or Indonesia include a positive affirmation of the role of religious plurality. However, this form of synthesis is fragile and can collapse under the influence of globalization and its weakening of the structures of nation-states, as is happening presently in Indonesia. In such situations religion may be transformed into an ideology to give legitimacy to the struggle against what is perceived to be a corrupt structure of governance.

3. Given the ambiguous impact of globalization on religion, it should not come as a surprise that we encounter very different responses from the religious communities themselves. In the discussion, a distinction is made between "anti-systemic" and "pro-systemic" responses (P. Beyer).

The first type is now generally being subsumed under the concept of "fundamentalism". While historically fundamentalism has its origins in evangelical Protestantism and the inner-Christian struggles to come to terms with modernization, the concept is now being used to describe those forms of religious resurgence in Islam, Hinduism, Buddhism and Judaism, as well as Christianity, which resist the impact of globalization. In many ways, fundamentalism is itself a product of the process of modernization. While its adherents often make the fullest use of the technological tools provided by the modern world and accept many of the features of globalization, they reject the explicit or implicit values that have guided the project of modernity. This is true especially with regard to secularization and to the role of religion.

Fundamentalism reclaims the absolute authority of a sacred tradition of belief and moral teaching. It rejects the specifically modern distinction between the secular and the sacred and seeks to bring religion back into the centre of the life of the community. However, fundamentalism should not be equated with a reactionary traditionalism. It rejects the seeming inevitability of the present dynamic of change and is determined to shape the world in a way that is different from the forces of modernity.

The other, pro-systemic type of response finds its expression in the emergence of the great variety of new religious movements which make deliberate use of the logic of globalization and intend to promote the values of universal harmony, peace and well-being. As examples one might point to the Unification Church with its origins in Korea, to several neo-Buddhist movements from Japan, the Hare-Krishna movement from India, the Church of Scientology, the neo-Pentecostal Universal Church of the Reign of God, and the many streams of the New Age movement. Different as they are, they are expressions of this new globalizing and often highly syncretistic religious reality. Many of them not only adapt easily to the situation of global plurality, but also engage in active competition to position themselves in the global context so as to gain influence, often by using economic and financial means.

From these globalizing new religious movements one has to distinguish what Robert Schreiter has called "global cultural or theological flows". "Global theological flows... are theological discourses that, while not uniform or systemic, represent a series of linked, mutually intelligible discourses that address the contradictions or failures of global systems."[20] While they are anti-systemic in addressing contradictions and failures in the global system, they also have the pro-systemic effect of creating a new global religious and spiritual consciousness, opening space for a truly global discourse and mobilizing people to exercise more effective religious influence on the directions of the process of globalization. Schreiter identifies such flows around four foci: liberation, feminism, ecology and human rights. None of these is exclusively linked to the Christian tradition. In fact, they represent crystallization points of global alliances of people or civic movements going beyond an anti-globalization stance and working for a transformation of the cultural patterns inherent in the process of globalization. They are agents and advocates of what Richard Falk has called a "politically engaged spirituality in an emerging global civil society" and protagonists of "globalization from below".[21]

4. It should not come as a surprise that globalization and religions challenge each other. Particularly the "world religions", like Christianity, Islam, Buddhism and also Hinduism, which have expanded through missionary efforts or migration from their regions of origin to diverse cultural contexts, represent a universal outlook on the whole of human life and its ultimate source of unity which can come into conflict with the secular universalism of globalization. Can this conflict be resolved?

For the defenders of the universality of the values of Western modernity and their spread by way of globalization this religious resurgence is a cause of apprehension and fear. It is seen as a potentially dangerous manifestation of fundamentalist attitudes rejecting globalization and confronting its agents and symbols. This is the background of the provocative thesis by Samuel Huntington that we are moving towards a "clash of civilizations".[22] Huntington does not share the expectation that the processes of modernization and globalization will lead to a levelling out of cultural differences. As a consequence of the religious resurgence, he rather sees the world becoming a multicultural, polycentric space with nine major civilizations, crystallizing around leading religions, the relationships between which bear a large potential for conflict. According to Huntington, the anticipated clash of civilizations will take the place of the previous ideological confrontation between the major power blocs. The recent confrontations between "Western civilization" and militant Islam seem to confirm his thesis.

Huntington's analysis has been strongly criticized both on historical and empirical grounds. He has, however, opened up an important discussion which is still continuing.[23] For it is obviously true that the religious resurgence is not unrelated to conflicts around power, resources and influence both within and between communities and states. Religion, together with culture and ethnicity, serves as a basis for collective identity in situations of political and social tension and disintegration.

> When communities identify themselves or are identified exclusively by their religion, situations become more explosive. Religion speaks for some of the deepest feelings and sensitivities of individuals and communities, it carries deep historic memories, and often appeals to universal loyalties, especially in the case of Christianity and Islam. And so religion comes to be seen as the cause of conflict and is often in fact an intensifier of conflicts whose causes are outside religion.[24]

The situation becomes particularly dangerous when conflicts which have very specific local roots are interpreted as manifestations of a global confrontation, e.g. between Christianity (or the West) and Islam. The globalization of communication rapidly spreads such stereotyped perceptions of the other community and then fosters a sense of irreconcilable antagonism and dangerously aggravates the conflict. There is therefore an urgent need to "de-globalize" such tensions and to focus attention again on the specific local causes of conflict which in most cases are political and/or economic rather than specifically religious in the sense of mutually exclusive religious cultures, life-styles and world-views. Such conflicts can only be resolved within the context itself.

In direct or indirect response to Huntington's thesis of the "clash of civilizations", the general assembly of the United Nations declared the year 2001 as a UN Year for the "Dialogue of Civilizations". This decision originated from a proposal by the Iranian state president Khatami, which was supported by the Conference of Islamic States. It gave renewed prominence to the efforts of inter-religious dialogue as a religious response to some of the challenges of globalization. In fact, more and more the United Nations, its specialized organizations, like UNESCO and ILO, and also international institutions or organizations, like the World Bank, the World Economic Forum or the InterAction Council, seek to enlist the support of "religious and spiritual leaders" in an effort to civilize globalization and give it an ethically more responsible face. This corresponds to the multiplication of inter-religious initiatives with global ambitions. The most widely known among these are the World Conference on Religion and Peace and the World Parliament of Religions. By furthering inter-religious dialogue on the global level, they intend to contribute to the building of a "culture of peace" which could help transform the conflicts and confrontations generated through the process of globalization.

The most prominent protagonist of this approach is Hans Küng, whose project for a "global ethic" has become the focal point of reference for many of the initiatives referred to above, in particular the "Declaration towards a Global Ethic" of the Parliament of the World's Religions of 1993 and the "Universal Declaration of Human Responsibilities" of the InterAction Council.[25] Küng is convinced that there will be no new world order without a new world ethic. He conceives of this "global ethic" as "a basic consensus on binding values, irrevocable criteria and basic attitudes which are affirmed by all religions despite dogmatic differences".[26] The core of this global ethic is the golden rule which, according to Küng, is acknowledged by all the world's religions. This core is then developed in terms of four irrevocable directives: the commitment to "a culture of non-violence and respect for life; a culture of solidarity and just economic order; a culture of tolerance and a life of truthfulness; and a culture of equal rights and partnership between men and women".[27]

Küng's advocacy for a global ethic has received a largely positive response from political and business leaders seeking moral and ethical guidance in managing globalization. The specific directives could also be affirmed by a more secular humanism as expressed in the report of the Commission on Global Governance.[28] However, Küng is convinced that only the spiritual authority of the great religions can generate the momentum to bring about the basic change of consciousness that will be necessary to overcome the global crisis.

Nevertheless, the question remains how the standards of this global ethic can be brought to bear effectively on social, political and economic life. Who are the agents to achieve this change of direction? Hans Küng places his hope in the common commitment and influence of political, economic, intellectual and religious leaders. But religions draw their genuine spiritual and moral strength from their closeness to the life of the people. Their moral power is rooted not in what religions share in common, which will always remain a fairly general minimal consensus, but in the "thickness" of their symbols, narratives and rituals, which distinguish them from one another.

Should it therefore be the aim of inter-religious dialogue to offer a global civilizing perspective, a global ethic or even a "global religion"? If inter-religious dialogue is to open ways of resolving and transforming communal and religious conflicts and thus to contribute to building a culture of peace, it would in fact seem more important to strengthen the ability of the adherents of different religious traditions to accept, respect and affirm their differences, not as mutually exclusive, but as enriching and complementing each other.

5. The main limitations of the approaches discussed here lie in their tendency to consider religion as a constructive, or

potentially destructive, function of the process of globalization. Depending on the assessment of globalization and its impact, religion will either be considered as a source of disturbance and even threat or as a civilizing and humanizing force. The terms of reference for this discussion are being provided by the globalization discourse, whether among academic intellectuals or among political and business leaders.

What is seldom, if ever, acknowledged is the fact that religions have a different and distinct approach to envisaging the whole of human existence. Globalization removes the limitations of space and time; the world becomes a single space, a "field of forces" (Schreiter), which are in constant movement but have no ultimate point of reference. For religious traditions the whole is conceived and given meaning by reference to a transcendent reality. Space and time in religious perspective are reminders of human finitude, which is sustained and will ultimately be transformed by the energy of life from beyond. True religious spirituality cannot be reduced to providing ethical and cultural resources for a globalized world. Religions, whatever their understanding of creation and eschatology, offer an alternative understanding of the global reality. Rooted as they are in human life in its rich diversity, they cannot easily be integrated into the universalizing and potentially totalizing perspective of globalization. The relationship between globalization and religion will thus remain one of tension marked by competing perspectives on global reality.

6. The Ecumenical Vision: An Alternative?

The previous chapter referred very generally to "religion" without entering into discussion as to how far this concept can be applied. It followed the usage in the social sciences, which employ abstract and generalizing concepts to order the diversity of features of human social life. Any closer analysis would, of course, show that there are obvious differences in the response of the world's religions to globalization, in particular between the Asian religions, especially Hinduism and Buddhism, on the one hand, and, on the other, the "Abrahamic", or monotheistic, religions of Judaism, Christianity and Islam. It would be important in any inter-religious dialogue on the challenges of globalization to enter more fully into these different world-views and their attitudes to plurality as well as to the relationship between religion, law and society. It is not, however, possible here to pursue that line of thought any further.

The Christian community has been actively involved in inter-religious dialogue and in shaping its potential responses to the challenges of globalization. Some would argue that in this present situation the emphasis should be placed on what is called "wider ecumenism", going deliberately beyond the scope of the ecumenical movement among Christian churches. Common attention, they feel, should be given to overcoming exclusivist or fundamentalist tendencies in order to avoid the potential "clash of civilizations". They are guided by the conviction that peace between the religions is a condition for peace among people. However, the previous analysis has tried to show that there is evidence as well for the fact that political, social and economic conflicts can aggravate tensions and antagonisms between religious communities. It could therefore be said with equal justification that without peace between people there will be no peace between religions. In any case, it will be important to avoid inter-religious dialogue being used simply as a means to manage the consequences of globalization.

Among the different religious responses to globalization, those from the Christian community deserve particular attention. In fact, the earliest and most articulate responses from a

religious perspective have come from the organized ecumenical movement of the Christian churches. At the same
time, Christian ecumenism is being sharply challenged by
globalization.

1. Historically, Christianity has been more deeply implicated
in the origins of globalization than any other religious community. The missionary vocation to carry the message of the
gospel to "the ends of the earth" has been part of the Christian self-understanding since apostolic times. While for long
centuries Christianity had adapted itself to the horizon of the
successive Christian empires, the missionary orientation
towards the whole world was revived in connection with
European colonial expansion. Through its missionary out-
reach, Christianity became an effective instrument in carry-
ing the spirit of modernity to other parts of the world, particularly with its work in the areas of education, health care
and economic development. Christianization and modernization went hand in hand. Christian mission became a civilizing project and was guided for a long time by the expectation
that, through the modernizing impact of the Western colonial
and missionary presence, traditional religions would gradu-
ally be transformed and thus the way prepared for the Christianization of the whole world.

> The missionary movement was the answer of Christian escha-
> tology to the new accessibility of the "ends of the earth"; fresh
> initiatives in the area of Christian social concern responded to
> the new visibility of the "world" nearby; and the rediscovery of
> the church and of the importance of the search for its unity
> reflected the broader cultural need to transform traditional
> separations into contemporary challenges. All this is unthink-
> able apart from the modern perspective of the "unity of
> humankind".[29]

The modern ecumenical movement has its origins in the
missionary revival in the second half of the 19th century. The
watchword of the Student Volunteer Movement for Mission
calling for the "evangelization of the world in this generation" also became a source of inspiration for the early ecu-

menical pioneers. At the same time, their initiatives were influenced by the emerging international consciousness at the turn from the 19th to the 20th century. Nathan Söderblom, one of the ecumenical pioneers, is quoted as exclaiming: "How wonderful it is that Christianity is international!" All the early ecumenical bodies and their leaders responded positively to the establishment of the League of Nations, believing that it was their task to give a "soul" to this "body" of new international institutions. Until the fundamental crises of the 1930s and 1940s, the ecumenical movement was guided by the conviction that the Christian ethos provided the only viable base for an international order, because it transcended national, ethnic or cultural loyalties.

The conviction that there was a particular Christian responsibility for shaping a viable human community also prompted the early ecumenical movement to struggle with the emerging secular culture and its scientific rationalism and materialism. A "spiritual conquest of the world" was called for and consideration was even given to the possibility of forming an alliance of all religions against the forces of secularization. This found its clearest expression in the resistance against the secular totalitarian ideologies of fascism and communism.

The total breakdown of all international order and its guiding values, and even more the communist take-over in China, which brought an abrupt end to the most ambitious Christian missionary enterprise, led to a fundamental reassessment of the nature of the Christian presence in the world. Leaving behind the Christendom heritage and the dreams of Christian supremacy in the religious field, ecumenical discussion returned to the eschatological orientation of its missionary origins. Faced with bewildering historical changes and discontinuities, it affirmed God as the Lord of world history. To discern God's action in history and thus, through participation in change, to contribute to the realization of God's shalom in the life of human community became the new interpretation of the ecumenical vocation. This found expression in the paradigm of "Christocentric universalism" (W.A. Visser 't Hooft), which served as the frame of reference for ecumenical reflection and action. At the Second Vatican Council, the Roman Catholic Church succeeded in leaving behind its earlier anti-modernist position and followed the ecumenical movement in its interpretation of world events in the perspective of salvation history. This enabled the ecumenical community in the World Council of Churches together with the Roman Catholic Church to affirm the unity of the church as a sign and instrument of the coming unity of humankind.[30]

This ecumenical convergence towards a characteristically modern vision of unity is now facing the challenge of globalization, because globalization presents itself, in the words of Bert Hoedemaker, as

> the secular realized *eschaton* of humankind: it promises universal and lasting salvation. As such, it is an extension of the specifically Western phenomenon of secularization: the "modern" functional rationality of politics and economy has institutionalized itself as a global network absorbing "the West" together with other parts of the world. Structural injustice – the focus in previous decades – is no longer mainly localized in the asymmetrical relations between the Western and the non-Western world; the divide itself has been globalized.

And he continues:

> Globalization is a deceptive form of "unity"; it suggests universal salvation while hiding and disguising division and fragmentation – a growing dichotomy between rich and poor, between global uniformity and local pluriformity – and a merciless attack on the "integrity of creation". In this respect it signals the failure of the "modern visions of unity" which had been so important for the genesis of the ecumenical movement. The ecumenical movement is deeply indebted to modernity and now finds itself called, by the logic of its own development, to rethink this heritage in a fundamental way.[31]

2. Unperturbed by this critical assessment, globalization is progressing and, in spite of its inner contradictions, seems to be able to bring about more effective forms of human unity than the Christian ecumenical movement. The churches are

still struggling to find ways of overcoming their historic divisions and responding together in common witness and service to the situation of a globalized world. In addition, statistical evidence would show that the organized ecumenical movement is reaching only a very limited segment of world Christianity which itself represents a religious minority among other minorities. In comparison with other world religions, the total share of Christians in the world population has not increased since the beginning of the 20th century. It still represents one-third of the total world population and, in absolute terms, has increased only in parallel to the general population growth. By comparison, the share of the Muslim community has grown from 12 percent at the beginning of the 20th century to presently 19 percent and it is expected to increase further in the coming decades. The Christian growth, along with overall population growth, is largely concentrated in the regions of the southern hemisphere and is most pronounced among the non-traditional Pentecostal or Evangelical communities. In comparison, the historic churches in the North which have been the main actors in the organized ecumenical movement are losing members and influence in their respective societies. At present it appears that the total number of Christians in non-traditional communities who have remained outside or have been strongly critical of the ecumenical movement is approximately equal to those belonging to the historic churches. Each represents about one quarter of world Christianity while the other half is represented by the Roman Catholic Church.

Of course such statistics are only of relative value, but they can help us to adopt a realistic and sober attitude to the universalizing claims of the ecumenical movement. In the context of reflections on ecumenical responses to globalization, it is of particular significance that the non-traditional Christian communities are growing fastest in the mega-cities or large metropolitan areas around the world, i.e. in those places which are most exposed to the impact of globalization. It is in these mega-cities and metropolitan regions that the ecumenical response to globalization will have to prove its validity, and it is therefore an important challenge to the ecumenical movement to open itself to these non-traditional communities.

Another aspect to be considered is the form of organization which the ecumenical movement has developed. Most ecumenical organizations, i.e. the World Council of Churches, the regional ecumenical organizations and the Christian world communions, base their membership on autonomous national church bodies, following the churches of the Protestant tradition, which have largely adopted the model of the nation-state for their own internal organization. Only the Roman Catholic Church and to a lesser degree the Orthodox churches and the Anglican communion have maintained the consciousness of the transnational identity of the Christian church.

Globalization has begun to weaken the basis of national sovereignty and of the authority of national governments.

The ecumenical organizations are therefore experiencing the same difficulty as intergovernmental organizations, like the United Nations, in keeping pace with a rapidly globalizing world situation. The organized ecumenical movement finds itself at a disadvantage over against the emerging networks and alliances of social movements and organizations in civil society, which have developed more flexible and effective forms of responding to globalization. The ecumenical movement will therefore have to develop and transform its organizational expressions in ways which facilitate the linking of the global and the local; which affirm diversity as an essential dimension of human community and not as a threat to unity; which open forms of participation beyond formal membership; which allow for ways of decision-making which allow room for dissent; and which integrate new ways of being church that do not follow the model of centralized national church structures.

3. Contemporary efforts to articulate an ecumenical response to globalization and to stimulate the search for alternative approaches can build on a substantial body of insights and

affirmations resulting from ecumenical discussion over the last thirty-five years since the Geneva conference on "Church and Society" in 1966. Initially the ecumenical community shared the expectation that the stimulation of economic growth and the transfer of technology would engender development and that the effects of this process would ultimately "trickle down" to the most disadvantaged members of the community. Soon, however, the ecumenical community felt compelled to sharpen its criteria by adding social justice and self-reliance as central requirements for a genuine process of development. Direct involvement in specific local initiatives by the churches' participation in development further enlarged the framework by emphasizing people's participation as a condition for human development. Following the Nairobi assembly in 1975, this led to the concept of a "just, participatory and sustainable society" as the framework guiding ecumenical efforts towards shaping a new international order in social, economic and political terms.

The emerging global threats to survival in the form of nuclear warfare and ecological deterioration challenged the Vancouver assembly in 1983 to initiate the ecumenical process for "Justice, Peace and the Integrity of Creation". This process, which met with the strongest response among the churches in Europe, was aimed at taking up a Christian confessional position against the threats to life and mobilizing the Christian community for acts of commitment and resistance. The world convocation on "Justice, Peace and the Integrity of Creation" in Seoul in 1990 accepted ten basic affirmations formulating the insights and convictions which had grown over several decades of ecumenical discussion. It committed itself to four acts of covenanting: on the debt crisis and the world economic order, on demilitarization and non-violence, on preserving the earth's atmosphere, and against racism and discrimination. Following this convocation, however, the ecumenical movement met strong resistance from those representing the churches and Christian communities in the South to any global analysis not starting from specific local experiences. The study document on

"Christian Faith and the World Economy Today", which was received by the central committee of the World Council of Churches and published in 1992, basically continued the global approach and had therefore limited impact.

The decade following the world convocation saw not only the rapid acceleration of the process of globalization but also a series of world conferences under UN auspices trying to come to terms with the new situation. Ecumenical partners and the World Council of Churches were involved in most of these conferences, from the Earth Summit in Rio de Janeiro in 1992, through the Social Summit in Copenhagen in 1995, to the World Conference against Racism in Durban in 2001. Through its participation in the activities of non-governmental organizations and social movements accompanying these world conferences, the ecumenical community received new impulses for its response to globalization. In particular the campaign to ban land mines and the Jubilee 2000 campaign for the cancellation of debts of the highly indebted poor countries, which were supported by worldwide networks of local and national initiatives and groups, including Christian communities, opened the way for new forms of active response to globalization. They enabled the ecumenical organizations to open their response to the vitality and imagination of local and national initiatives and thus to move on from the previous predominance of a global analytical approach.

4. In preparation for the Harare assembly, two WCC publications tried to summarize the insights emerging from previous efforts to come to terms with the challenges of globalization. In his book *Faith in a Global Economy*, Rob van Drimmelen, who for more than a decade had been the WCC staff member responsible for the area of economy and justice, provides a competent introduction to the subject for a wider Christian audience. He deals with the features of the globalizing economy with a view to finding responses from the basic tenets of the Christian faith. His introduction focuses on developments in the fields of international trade,

transnational corporations, international finance, work, employment and unemployment, land and the functions of the market for economic growth. Richard Dickinson, in his background study on *Economic Globalization: Deepening Challenge for Christians*, summarizes the discussions and reflections of three ecumenical consultations on globalization held in preparation for the Harare assembly. He offers an analysis of "five basic realities of globalization", i.e. the concentration of corporate power, the movements of speculative financial capital, the impact of computer technology and its applications, the widening disparities between rich and poor, and the power of a "free market" ideology. Over against these realities, he formulates basic ecumenical affirmations, drawing on statements of WCC assemblies and ecumenical conferences, and exposes the ideological character of the prevailing form of economic globalization and its destructive impact on the lives of human communities.[32]

Both publications end with an affirmation of Christian hope in response to globalization, which receives particular inspiration from the biblical models of the sabbath and the jubilee year focusing on the restoration of right relationships in the human community. In the gospel proclamation of Jesus, the sabbath and the jubilee model become interpretations for his announcement of the messianic kingdom (cf. Luke 4:18-19). Van Drimmelen writes:

> This messianic hope is an inspiration for those who go against the tide and who do not want to give up. It is a reminder that the status quo is temporary and calls for imagination in looking for solutions to the problems of today. In a time of crass materialism when so many seem to be obsessed by possessions, the jubilee vision calls for cultural disobedience by putting limits on the frenzy of acquisitiveness. The sabbath, the sabbath year and jubilee year emphasize that "to be" is not "to have", but to provide justice to the poor. They resist the logic of the market based on endless accumulation and competition. Over against the right of the strongest they put the right of the weakest and the poor. Over against the inclination to dominate the earth they put the notion of dominion and patrimony.[33]

The Harare assembly of the WCC in 1998 responded to the challenge of globalization with its "jubilee call to end the stranglehold of debt on impoverished peoples"[34] and with a set of policy recommendations on globalization. This latter statement begins with the following affirmations:

> Globalization is not simply an economic issue. It is a cultural, political, ethical and ecological issue... The vision behind globalization includes a competing vision to the Christian commitment to the oikoumene, the unity of humankind and the whole inhabited earth... Although globalization is an inescapable fact of life, we should not subject ourselves to the vision behind it, but strengthen our alternative ways towards visible unity in diversity, towards an oikoumene of faith and solidarity. The logic of globalization needs to be challenged by an alternative way of life of community in diversity. Christians and churches should reflect on the challenge of globalization from a faith perspective and therefore resist the unilateral domination of economic and cultural globalization. The search for alternative options to the present economic system and the realization of effective political limitations and corrections to the process of globalization and its implications are urgently needed.

Apart from many specific issues mentioned in the critical response to economic globalization, the statement places special emphasis on creating effective institutions of global governance to control the unaccountable power of transnational corporations and on the close coordination of work on economic and ecological issues.

The policy recommendations on globalization were accompanied by a background document under the title "Resisting Domination – Affirming Life: The Challenge of Globalization", which was included in the assembly report to provide additional resources for continuing ecumenical work on the issues of globalization. The document points to the concentration of power, to the dramatic reality of unequal distribution of power and wealth, to poverty and exclusion, and to the contradictions, tensions and anxieties arising from the process of globalization. It clearly exposes the neo-liberal ideology as the driving force behind economic globalization.

Against this background, the document interprets the pastoral, ethical, theological and spiritual challenge which globalization poses to the churches and the ecumenical movement. In this context, it draws attention to the dimension of the catholicity of the church as an essential point of reference for a theological response to globalization.

> The traditional concept of the catholicity of the church deserves renewed attention. The notion and praxis of catholicity can be understood as an early form of Christian response to the imperial form of unity that was shaped and represented by the Roman empire. Such an alternative option to the imperial power is of relevance for the affirmation of the ecumenical dimension in the life of the churches in the context of globalization.

Referring to the biblical jubilee vision, the document calls for a fundamental reshaping of the economic system to affirm God's gift of life that is threatened in so many ways. It then develops this life-centred vision by taking up once again the theme of the Canberra assembly "Come, Holy Spirit – Renew the Whole Creation".

> According to the creation stories of the Bible, the earth was meant to be home for all living creatures, which live in different spaces, but linked to each other in a web of relationships. The human community is placed within the wider community of the earth, which is embedded in God's household of life. It is this vision of a truly ecumenical earth that challenges the ecumenical movement to search for new ways of revitalizing and protecting the communities of indigenous peoples and of the marginalized and excluded, participating in resistance against the growing domination of economic globalization, and engaging itself in the building of a culture of peace and just relationships, a culture of sharing and solidarity.

This life-centred vision calls the ecumenical community to promote participation, equity, accountability and sufficiency as essential requirements for an alternative to globalization.

The document finally acknowledges that, in the context of globalization, churches and Christians often have compromised their convictions and given in to the temptations of power, influence and wealth. It therefore calls on the WCC "to strengthen the ecumenical dimension in the life of the churches and provide space necessary for dialogue and mutual up-building towards a common witness by the churches locally, regionally and internationally". It encourages the new central committee and all member churches "to develop a more coherent approach to the challenges of globalization, with a focus on life in dignity and trust in sustainable communities".

The Programme Guidelines Committee of the Harare assembly reinforced this thrust by identifying globalization as one of the overall themes to receive particular attention in the work of the WCC in the period ahead. It emphasized that

> the challenge of globalization to the churches must be seen first and foremost as a theological and spiritual challenge. The love of God, expressed fully in Christ, reveals a vision of fullness of life for all; the emerging global economy projects a vision of limitless material gratification for those who can afford it. Thus the churches are called to witness to and embody God's intention for the world in the face of growing globalization and the values which underlie it...
>
> While the term "globalization" is often used ambiguously and while many of the features of the process characterized as "globalization" are ambivalent, it is evident that the elements of the new global context which the term describes require concentrated attention from the WCC in the coming years. The Council is invited to take an ecumenical approach to globalization in a perspective that identifies and links together issues and brings out the biblical imperatives. International and national governance, consumption and production patterns, financial systems and trade, and the impact of these on national debt and people's rights to land and sustainable livelihood should receive particular attention.

The central committee confirmed this direction for its programme given by the assembly by adopting "Common Witness and Service amidst Globalization" as one of four themes in an overarching framework for the Council's future work. To the aspects of globalization needing particular attention the central committee adds the growth of religious plurality and the call to explore with partners of other faith communities "how common commitments to human rights and dignity can be translated into a global framework of values to which all can subscribe".[35] Monitoring the specific initiatives of the WCC in the area of globalization, the central committee at its meeting in 2001 urged again that "the member churches and the WCC develop a comprehensive ecumenical theological analysis of economic globalization and its impact on the churches and on society, and provide a theological basis for the search for alternatives".[36] More particularly, the central committee recommended that the

WCC [should] focus on searching for alternatives to economic globalization based on Christian values in the following three areas:
- the transformation of the current market economy to embrace equity and values that reflect the teachings and example of Christ;
- development of just trade;
- the promotion of a just financial system, free of debt bondage, corrupt practices and excessive speculative profit making.[37]

These recommendations by the central committee describe succinctly the framework of present ecumenical efforts to formulate critical responses to economic globalization in cooperation with a broad network of ecumenical organizations and agencies. While the critical focus on economic globalization has continued and even been intensified, the above recommendation has yet to be followed up and attention has yet to be given to developing a "comprehensive ecumenical theological analysis" and the articulation of a "theological basis for the search for alternatives" binding together the concerns for global governance, economic justice and ecological integrity.

5. The effort to provide a theological basis for the search for alternatives to the present form of globalization must begin from a fresh understanding of the way the biblical tradition talks about the whole world and its comprehensive

unity. The three following biblical themes can serve as examples.

(1) The Hebrew Bible opens with a highly symbolic account of the primeval history of the world and humanity. This account closes with the story of the *Tower of Babel* (Gen. 11:1ff.). The story describes how primeval humanity tried to preserve their unity manifested in a common language by gathering in one place and building a fortified city and "a tower with its top in the heavens". In the language of myth it is an account of the eternal dream of all dominant empires to secure themselves over against any outside force which could challenge or fragment their unity, even over against God, the transcendent "other". They want to be fully autonomous, making a name for themselves. The story, through the intervention of God, who confuses their language so that they can no longer understand each other, points to the inherent fragility of this imperialistic dream. Precisely by denying their own dependency and vulnerability, they end up a fragmented, dispersed community in non-communication.

But then the biblical account continues with a new departure, i.e. God's call to Abraham to leave his secure place and to go into an unknown future (Gen. 12:1ff.). This stands in contrast to the story of Babel. God will make Abraham's name great, God will bless him, and in him "all the families of the earth shall be blessed" (v.3). Over against the affirmation of autonomy and the denial of dependency in the story of Babel, we find here the utter dependency of Abraham upon the guidance and blessing of God. In contrast to the imperial dream of unification, we see here the blessing of God for all the families of the earth. It is this blessing which brings about a sustainable unity of humankind. In that sense, the true counterpart to the story of Babel is the event of Pentecost, where the blessing from God comes upon the assembly of people from all corners of the known world in the form of the gift of the Holy Spirit who enables them to hear the good news being proclaimed and to understand it each and everyone in their own language. Thus, the diversity of languages and cultures is not abolished but affirmed through the restoration of communication. A sustainable human community is a community of communication. The spirit of God is the energy of life in community and communication.

(2) The second way in which the biblical tradition conceives the world as a comprehensive whole is represented by the *eschatological perspective* of the prophetic proclamation. Biblical prophecy, from the great prophets of Israel up to the apocalyptic visions of the book of Revelation, places images of hope over against the claims of political and economic power. The prophets discern the vulnerability and inner contradictions of the ambitions of human power and confront them with images of hope which envision a new heaven and a new earth (Isa. 65:17; Rev. 21:1), the great "jubilee" (Isa. 61:1ff.; Luke 4:18f.), the new Jerusalem as the symbol of sustainable community (Ezek. 40; Isa. 65:19ff.), the city coming down from heaven, not built by human hands, into which the nations and the kings of the earth will bring their glory (Rev. 21:2ff.,22ff.). The parables through which Jesus announced the coming reign of God also stand in this prophetic tradition. The global unity of all things in heaven and on earth becomes a reality in expectation of the end time, when God's plan for the fullness of time will be fulfilled "to gather up all things in Christ" (Eph. 1:10). It is this prophetic, eschatological perspective from the end which has sustained the true biblical universalism.

(3) The third essential element which was also mentioned in the background document presented to the Harare assembly is the understanding of the earth and all that is within it as being God's *creation* (Ps. 24:1). It is important to recall that this widening of the scope of biblical faith to embrace the whole world as God's creation, dependent on the Creator and sustained by God in its life, has emerged as a response to the utter disillusionment with the political aspirations of Israel and doubts about God's faithfulness to the covenants from Abraham to David. The confession of God as the Creator of heaven and earth, of all that is and lives, transcends the claims of all total systems, whether political, economic or ideological, and unmasks them as false pretensions of human

power. God has not created the world at the beginning and then left it to its own fate: God and the world remain bound together. The world as God's creation remains dependent on the power of God's blessing. The world is not a closed global system under the inescapable rule of the laws of nature or history. The world is open towards God and no power of the world can destroy this fundamental relationship to the Creator. God the Creator remains the Lord also of the invisible powers and principalities (Col. 1:15ff.), and so the "new creation" becomes another expression of eschatological hope trusting in God's faithfulness (2 Cor. 5:17).

This creation perspective is of particular importance for an ecumenical response to globalization. The vision of an "ecumenical earth" is the alternative to the vision of globalization based on the pretensions of the global market. God's creation provides the space for all life and all spaces are linked with each other in a web of relationships sustaining and supporting each other. In the perspective of the Creator, the earth is a community of communities and humanity is endowed with the capacity and the responsibility to be the trustee caring for this web of relationships. To see this intricate web as a whole, to envisage the integrity of God's creation, is the perspective of faith, a faith which is rooted in the promise that God's salvation not only means fullness of life for the human community but the restoration of creation to its goodness. It is only as the ecumenical movement re-appropriates this perspective that it will be able to meet the challenge of globalization.

6. A further element of a more developed theological basis guiding the search for alternatives has already been mentioned in the background document on globalization presented to the Harare assembly, i.e. the concept of the *catholicity* of the church. Robert Schreiter, in his reflections on globalization, points in the same direction when he says:

Theology must be able to interact with globalization theory out of its own internal history and resources and not be simply reactive to it. It seems to me that the concept of *catholicity* may be the theological concept most suited to developing a theological view of theology between the global and the local in a world church.[38]

It is therefore not surprising that already in the context of the earlier ecumenical discussions about the inter-relationship between the unity of the church and the unity of humankind, the traditional concept of the catholicity of the church received new attention. It is generally agreed that the notion of the catholicity of the church includes two distinct, yet inter-related dimensions, i.e. the reference to the universality of the church, as well as to the fullness of its life in Christ, or the orthodoxy of its confession of faith. To the extent that a given church confesses and lives the same faith that is confessed in all other churches, it is the catholic church in the given place. It is a church in the full sense of the meaning of *ecclesia* and not a territorial sub-division of a larger body. The catholicity of the church, in the sense of its universality, is rooted in the fact that all churches draw on the same source of faith, i.e. God's gift of new life in Jesus Christ.

The ecumenical discussions aiming at a re-appropriation of the concept of catholicity have emphasized the eschatological dialectic inherent in the concept. The catholicity of the church is first of all God's gift in Christ; the koinonia expressed locally and universally is rooted in the Trinitarian communion of the Father with the Son through the Holy Spirit. The church is already experiencing its catholicity now in the sense of the fullness of new life and the universality of its communion, but the church is itself to be understood as a sign and instrument for that new community when God will bring all people together in God's kingdom, in the heavenly city, in a new heaven and earth based on just relationships.

In this sense the Uppsala assembly (1968) presented a new understanding of catholicity which is important for meeting the challenge of globalization.

Since Christ lived, died and rose again for all mankind [sic!], catholicity is the opposite of all kinds of egoism and particularism. It is the quality by which the church expresses the fullness, the integrity and totality of life in Christ... Catholicity is the gift of the Spirit, but it is also a task, a call and an engagement.[39]

The same report later affirms that this renewed discovery of catholicity

calls the churches in all places to realize that they belong together and are called to act together. In a time when human interdependence is so evident, it is the more imperative to make visible the bonds which unite Christians in universal fellowship...[40]

The eschatological dialectic between the reality of the gift of catholic communion already now and the expectant hope for its final fulfilment places the search for the catholicity of the church in missionary perspective: the church is God's instrument in preparing the way for the final "catholic" communion in God's kingdom.[41] The church, therefore, is called to open itself up to the world, to all of creation, and to realize the gift of its catholicity day by day. This is the vision of the oikoumene, of the unity of the church in solidarity with the search for viable human community and for the integrity of creation. This is the source for an alternative to the vision of globalization, for alternative ways towards visible unity in diversity, towards an oikoumene of faith and solidarity. The earlier ecumenical reflections on catholicity can help to develop and sharpen this alternative. There is, first, the warning not to betray the gift of catholicity by confusing it with other solidarities or communities. The process of globalization, which began in the field of economy and finance, is more and more invading the realms of communication, culture and also religion. In adapting themselves to the demands of global society, Christian churches and communities run the danger of betraying the gift of catholicity, which calls into question all manifestations of human power. The arrogance of power and the pride in one's own confessional community were identified early on as forms of the betrayal of catholicity, as were the tendencies of sectarian or fundamentalist withdrawal, or the position of a relativizing pluralism.

Catholicity is to be realized in the midst of the ambiguities of the process of globalization, not as a total rejection but as a transforming dynamic.

The decisive test for the church in living out its catholicity is the way in which it responds to and integrates the diversities in the human community in its own life. The churches' claim to catholicity will only be credible if they are able in their own life to transcend all forms of segregation and discrimination, if they overcome the exclusiveness of race and class, gender and (dis)ability and resist economic and political exploitation. Catholicity calls the churches to provide space for diversity, to make room for all conditions of human life and for open mutual confrontation of different interests and convictions.

It is for this reason that there exists an inner link between catholicity and conciliarity. In fact, the catholicity of the church is actualized in conciliar forms of life. It is certainly not by accident that the early forms of conciliarity were developed and implemented in the church of the first centuries at the very time when an early form of "globalization" was beginning to emerge on the political level in the Roman empire. The conciliar ways of maintaining communion between churches, separated not only by distance and history but also by culture and language, represent at least an indirect way of resisting the pressures of submitting to the dominant political model. Since then conciliarity as a permanent feature in the life of the church as communion has been differently expressed according to varying social, cultural and historical conditions. However, the conciliar form of life has always been a point of resistance against power structures in church and society. It is the form in which the Christian community can recognize, on the local as well as the regional and universal levels, diversity and plurality without giving in to relativism.

The strength of this "catholic" alternative to globalization is rooted in the ability to hold together the local and the global or universal. They are inseparably inter-related. It is here that the proposal by Robert Schreiter for a "new catholicity" takes on its significance.

It seems to me that a renewed and expanded concept of catholicity may well serve as a theological response to the challenge of globalization. It can provide a theological framework out of which the church might understand itself and its mission under changed circumstances. Faced with the diversity of cultures and the implications of taking them seriously, and the challenge of maintaining the unity and integrity of the church worldwide, the eschatological sense of catholicity, so important to the Orthodox and many Protestant churches, and reaffirmed by Roman Catholics at the Second Vatican Council, takes on new salience at the interface of the global and the local. This is echoed in some reflections on catholicity: Avery Dulles speaks of catholicity as the ability to hold things together in tension with one another; Peter Schineller speaks of it as a tentativeness, anticipating the whole.[42]

Indeed, this understanding of the catholicity of the church represents a very significant approach to spelling out the link between the local and the global. What is essential is the insistence that neither the local nor the global can claim priority: they have their validity only in relationship with one another. It is here that the eschatological perspective is of particular importance, because it protects the church from the pressures of both localism and fundamentalism and provides a strategy of resistance against the impact of globalization and conformity to the demands of global unity. The fullness of catholicity will only be revealed at the end of time. Some advocates of globalization want to make us believe that we can disregard or overcome the limitations of space and time, the conditions of human finiteness. The eschatological perspective reminds us that the catholicity of the church can be actualized only as a communion of local churches conditioned by the particularities of a given "place" or "context". It remains bound to the categories of space and time, and that means to the basic elements of human existence.

7. Our analysis of the features of globalization, the three biblical references and the brief reflection on catholicity have pointed to the fact that a developed theological basis for responding to globalization will have to address the issue of

power. Globalization is the result of excessive concentration of power and its largely uncontrolled use. To offer theological and ethical considerations on the uses of power in the ecumenical movement today requires us to take into account the fact that power is beginning to be dissociated from the traditional framework of the state and is manifesting itself more and more as economic, intellectual, or media power largely beyond the reach of governments and the established procedures for exercising controls. The dominant model of power in the globalized world today is the model of business management, emphasizing power as the ability to implement decisions in order to maintain competitiveness in the market. A theological analysis of this logic of power will have to place the exercise of power once again in its social context.

Power can be understood as the accumulation of means in the pursuit of particular ends. Means can be capital, property, armaments, knowledge, status or communication, all of which can be turned into instruments of power. The accumulation of means is the result of social interaction. Globalization is the result of a technological revolution in the area of means, in particular regarding communication and information processing. The development of these means, their accumulation and the control of access to them, opens new sources of power, in particular if they are being used for the unlimited accumulation of money and capital.

But there is also the question of the definition of ends, which is also the result of social interaction. The fact that the accumulation of these new means has often become an end in itself raises the basic question of the legitimacy of power. Legitimacy is dependent on the criterion whether power serves acceptable and commonly agreed ends. The definition of ends finds expression in culturally agreed values and in legal norms. State power traditionally established its legitimacy by following "due process" and observing legal and constitutional conditions placed on the exercise of power. In the new situation of a diffusion of power over a diversity of actors, these traditional ways of establishing legitimacy can no longer exclude the danger of either an inappropriate use of means or a socially destructive pursuit of ends. The fact that certain uses of power are legal is no longer a guarantee of their legitimacy.

It is at this point that the churches and other organizations in civil society enter the picture. In view of the erosion of traditional values and moral norms as a consequence of the process of globalization and the explicit disregard of concerns for the common good under the rule of the logic of the market, the new forms of exercising power face an increasing lack of legitimacy. This is being recognized more and more by many of the global actors who are turning to the churches and religious communities with the expectation that they might help in restoring a sense of commonly acceptable ends to guide the use of the accumulated means. In fact, there is such an abundance of means of potential power that they are beginning to block and interfere with each other unless their use be directed towards constructive and humanly responsible ends.

Defining the ends therefore becomes in itself a new source of power. The power struggles in a globalized world will not centre so much on the means and the access to them, but on symbolic power, i.e. the capacity to articulate ends which provide meaning and social coherence. The symbolic power inherent in the project of modernity, i.e. its promise of unlimited progress and of happiness and well-being for the greatest number, has been exhausted. There is a widespread search today for powerful symbols of hope transcending the threats to life resulting from the process of globalization. Therefore it is important to reappropriate the biblical symbols of hope already referred to.

However, the theological analysis has to be pushed further. All symbolism of power ultimately has religious roots. In the Christian perspective, God is the ultimate model and source of power. There is therefore an intimate relationship between the dominant images of God and the way in which power is exercised in human community. The first and basic affirmation of the world convocation on "Justice, Peace and the Integrity of Creation" in Seoul in 1990 stated that "all exercise of power is accountable to God". This affirmation was developed in the following paragraph:

> The world belongs to God. Therefore, all forms of human power and exercise of authority should serve God's purposes in the world and are answerable to the people on whose behalf they are exercised. Those who wield power – economic, political, military, social, scientific, cultural, legal, religious – must be stewards of God's justice and peace. In Christ, God's power is demonstrated in redemptive suffering, as compassionate love which identifies itself with broken and suffering humanity. This empowers people to proclaim the message of liberation, love and hope which offers new life, to resist injustice and to struggle against the powers of death.[43]

In the effort to push the theological analysis of power further, it may be important to recall the response of the early church when, in the Arian crisis, it was confronted with the theological legitimization of imperial power in the form of "political monotheism". Over against this symbolism, binding together one God and one emperor, the oneness of the church and the oneness of the empire, the ecumenical councils of Nicea and Constantinople affirmed the confession of God as the Holy Trinity, i.e. as the communion of the distinct persons of the Father, the Son and the Holy Spirit. The fundamental symbolism of power, therefore, is no longer monarchical rule, but a communion in diversity, exercising power in mutual love, sharing and communication. The logic of accumulation and domination is replaced by the logic of sharing and self-giving. The decisive biblical symbols of divine power, therefore, are the blessing which sustains life, the cross of Jesus Christ as the victory over the powers of death, and the Holy Spirit, the giver of life and the source of communion and communication. Any ecumenical theological response to the concentration of power in the context of globalization and the critical discussion about its legitimacy should return to this alternative biblical symbolism of power in order to give shape to an alternative vision which can face up to the pretensions of globalization. In this alternative vision the love of power is replaced by the power of love.

II
Towards a Culture of Reconciliation and Peace

1. Reconsidering Peace and Justice

The ecumenical movement has been committed from the beginning to the task of peace-building and reconciliation. There is an accumulated body of insights and convictions which remains an important guide in confronting the contemporary challenges to find peaceful ways of resolving conflicts. Much of the ecumenical reflection and action about war and peace over the past decades has been shaped by the antagonism of the cold-war period and particularly the threat of nuclear confrontation; but through its active participation in the struggles for social justice and liberation the ecumenical movement was led to reaffirm the biblical, prophetic insight that peace is the fruit of justice. The threats to peace do not arise only from military aggression but equally from hunger, oppression and injustice. This was linked with an increasingly critical assessment of all purely military systems of security, especially the doctrine of "national security". The statement of the Vancouver assembly of the WCC (1983) on "Peace and Justice" remains the authoritative summary of the critical insights gained during this period.[1]

The Vancouver assembly also provided the inspiration for the conciliar process on "Justice, Peace and the Integrity of Creation". This process reopened the earlier discussion on violence and non-violence in the struggle for social justice which had been marked by controversy over ecumenical support to liberation movements struggling against racism and apartheid. Strong voices emerged during the JPIC process arguing for a "privileged option for non-violence" as the basis for the Christian peace witness. This was echoed at the world convocation on "Justice, Peace and the Integrity of Creation" at Seoul in 1990 when it formulated the commitment "to practise non-violence in all our personal relationships, to work for the banning of war as a legally recognized means of resolving conflict, and to press governments for the establishment of an international legal order of peacemaking". The commitment was underlined and strengthened in an act of covenanting "for a culture of active non-violence which is life-promoting and is not a withdrawal from situations of violence and oppression, but is a way to work for justice and liberation".[2]

Today we realize that the changes in the world after 1989 have profound implications for our ecumenical witness for peace and reconciliation.[3] Our analysis of the process of globalization has already pointed to some of the new features and, in fact, it was only after 1989 that the dynamic of global capitalism began to develop without restraint with the implications of weakening the structures of governance on the national and international level and giving rise to new conflicts around ethnic, cultural and also religious identity. Initially, however, it had seemed that a new period of peace and stability had begun.

Over against a purely Euro-centric view, the year 1989-90 must be considered as one of those epochal years with worldwide repercussions. While the events were initially centred in Europe, they do not only signify the collapse of the system of state socialism in Central and Eastern Europe. That period also saw the beginning of the end of apartheid in South Africa, which has meanwhile been sealed with the adoption of a new, non-racial constitution. The way for peace agreements in Central America was also opened up, but we have also seen the suppression of the democracy movement in the People's Republic of China. The changes in Europe have found their significant expression in the "Charter for a New Europe", adopted at the summit meeting of the Conference on Security and Cooperation in Europe in Paris in November 1990. This was accompanied by the first ever process of genuine disarmament, going far beyond the traditional agreements on arms control. In many other parts of the world, these changes have found expression in determined moves towards democratization and in new expectations regarding the role of the United Nations for peace-building and conflict resolution. The end of the cold war has ended the situation of bipolar confrontation which had characterized not only the European and North Atlantic political scene for several decades, but which had been the framework for international politics in general. The question of an international order of peace is no longer the object of academic discussion alone, but has moved into the centre of international politics.

However, the Gulf war, following only shortly after the historic events in Europe, revealed clearly that the move from confrontation to cooperation was neither automatic nor without ambiguity. The debate about the Gulf war at the Canberra assembly of the WCC (1991) demonstrated that, despite the commitments at the Seoul convocation, the churches were not yet in a position to give a coherent answer to the question of how to respond to international conflicts without resorting to war and in ways that promote peace with justice. Many of the present international political tensions and unresolved conflicts have their origin in the rather ambiguous political responses at that time.

The dilemma has been exacerbated by the more recent violent conflicts in the former Yugoslavia and in several African countries. The resurgence of nationalism, the experience of genocidal violence and of ethnic cleansing and the inability of the United Nations to live up to its role of maintaining world peace, have created a situation of uncertainty and confusion. There is no clarity either politically or ethically about the definition of the problems and consequently about appropriate solutions. What is most disconcerting is the fact, already discussed in our reflections on globalization, that in many of these conflicts national identity, ethnicity and religious loyalty have begun to form an explosive mix which seems to make the problems almost insoluble. The challenge of terrorism has dramatically exposed this situation. While it is true that only few of the post-cold war conflicts are centred directly on religion, it is equally true that religious loyalties have been used and manipulated for political ends, and religious communities, whether Christian, Muslim or otherwise, have largely been unable to defend themselves against this distortion of the integrity of their faiths. This fact certainly underlines that religious communities, including the Christian churches, are as much part of the problem as they might be able to be part of its solution.

It is significant that in this situation of resurgence of violent conflicts the central committee of the WCC at its meeting in Johannesburg in January 1994 decided to launch a
WCC Programme to Overcome Violence. But this renewed
ecumenical commitment to peaceful resolution of conflict
was put to a severe test during the following four years.[4] In
April 1994 the world was shocked by the genocide in
Rwanda, the beginning of a long-drawn-out conflict in the
entire region of the Great Lakes in Central Africa. In September 1994, the war in Bosnia-Herzegovina entered into its
most brutal phase, marked especially by the practice of "ethnic cleansing". While the peace mission in Somalia had to be
terminated at the end of 1994 before having reached its
objectives, the call for a "humanitarian intervention" in the
Balkan war became stronger, a call in which the ecumenical
community joined.

It was in this situation that the central committee of the
WCC in 1995 adopted a message on the conflict in the former Yugoslavia in which it acknowledged "a widening gap
between differing Christian attitudes to war and peace, the
use of sanctions, and whether violence can be justified as a
last resort in the pursuit of peace".[5] A year later, the central
committee received with appreciation a "Note on the Contemporary Role of the Church in International Affairs" which
reviewed the painful ecumenical debate and asked: "What
alternatives has the church to offer to violence as a response
to conflict? What can the church do to lower or eradicate the
incidence of violence in society? How can the churches and
Christians strengthen their capacity to remain in dialogue on
deeply divisive social and political issues?"[6] In response, the
document pointed to the recent attempt to develop "criteria
for determining the applicability and effectiveness of sanctions"[7] and to the launching of the Programme to Overcome
Violence. But questions still remained: "Have we been effective in moving from declaration and affirmation to action?
Have we spoken in such a way that what we say can be heard
by and make a difference to the churches? Have we helped to
make the universal Christian witness meaningful and potent

in a confused world?" (p.176). All of these challenges came into even sharper focus as a consequence of the Kosovo conflict and the military intervention by NATO. That intervention clearly violated international law, but was officially justified as necessary to defend the human rights of the Kosovo Albanian population, who had become the target of a policy of "ethnic cleansing" by the Serbian authorities.

In trying to find a common response to these intractable conflicts and to remain faithful to the ecumenical commitment to peaceful resolution of conflict, the words of the prophet Jeremiah have often come to mind: "They have healed the wound of my people lightly, saying 'peace, peace' when there is no peace" (Jer. 6:14). In fact, one of the basic affirmations of the ecumenical movement since earliest times has been that a durable peace can only be built on the basis of justice. The Vancouver assembly in 1983, in its statement on "Peace and Justice", said:

> Peace is not just the absence of war. Peace cannot be built on foundations of injustice. Peace requires a new international order based on justice for and within all the nations, and respect for the God-given humanity and dignity of every person. Peace is, as the prophet Isaiah has taught us, the effect of righteousness... The ecumenical approach to peace and justice is based on the belief that without justice for all everywhere we shall never have peace anywhere.[8]

However, it is precisely this conviction which has been put to the test in these recent conflicts. Is not "humanitarian intervention" in the defence of human rights an act of justice? And, on the other hand, are there not ever more situations where an end of violent confrontation is the essential condition for any attempt to build a more just order? How can ecumenical solidarity with the victims of injustice and violence be practised if the distinction between victims and perpetrators becomes blurred, when the former victims become perpetrators themselves? And how can the work of reconciliation begin if both sides understand themselves as victims of injustice? The document from the central committee in 1996 which was quoted earlier says:

> After decades of dealing with what seemed to be clear-cut
> issues of right and wrong, the churches have been confronted
> with new moral and ethical dilemmas. What do we do when
> there is no "just" solution, when the "legitimate" claims for jus-
> tice by several parties to a conflict deny justice to the other?
> What moral criteria do we apply when to judge the one and
> absolve the other is in itself an act of injustice? (p.181)

As the same document reminds us, we are still deeply
conditioned by thinking in categories of the cold war based
on the clear identification of an enemy and the confrontation
of absolute good with absolute evil. The confrontational
logic of war, i.e. the tendency to solve a problem or conflict
by establishing the dominance of one position over the other,
has shaped relationships in the political, social and even cultural field more deeply than we are ready or able as yet to
acknowledge. It has, in particular, produced an understanding of conflicts in terms of a zero sum game in which gaining power by one side necessarily means that the other side
loses. The expectation and the fear that the "winner takes all"
is one of the hidden reasons for the interminable conflicts in
Africa.

The transformation of violence into peaceful conflict resolution has to begin by questioning the deeply rooted cultural
inclination to think in opposites. Instead, we must raise
awareness of the dimensions of reciprocity and mutuality.
Violence cannot be overcome by imposing superior power
and enforcing obedience and submission, since violence is in
itself an expression of the confrontational logic of power.
The effort to build a culture of peace, therefore, has to be
rooted in an understanding of power as a resource for the life
of the community which increases as it is shared. Peaceful
resolution of conflict is possible only when the win-lose
model is transformed into a dynamic where both sides
emerge as having won.

This has implications also for our understanding of justice. Much of the ecumenical discussion has been shaped by
a punitive and forensic concept of justice aimed at establishing right and punishing the wrong-doer, at the expense of

promoting justice in the sense of healing and restoring the life of the community. Too often the appeal to justice and the law has been used as a political instrument to punish those perceived to be enemies instead of promoting justice as the cooperative effort to resolve a conflict or to heal the wounds of history. The central committee document of 1996 highlights the experience since the Canberra assembly, which

> shows that the law alone is insufficient to bring lasting justice or durable peace... Jesus came to fulfil the law, but at the same time to free us from bondage to an absolutist system of law based on retribution. His message of forgiveness has shown itself anew to be not just a requirement of the faith, but a political necessity, if we are ever to overcome ancient enmities, our tendency to pursue justice on our own terms and at any price, and our penchant to resort to violence in the name of peace and justice. We have learned that there are times when there can be no justice if there is not some peace. (p.182)

Reviewing the work of the WCC on justice and peace during this period, the Harare assembly (1998) not only adopted a policy statement on human rights but identified "non-violence and reconciliation" as one of the overall themes for WCC activities during the years ahead. The report of the Programme Guidelines Committee stated:

> There is need to bring together the work on gender and racism, human rights and transformation of conflict in ways that engage the churches in initiatives for reconciliation that build on repentance, truth, justice, reparation and forgiveness. The Council should work strategically with the churches on these issues to create a culture of non-violence, linking and interacting with other international partners and organizations, and examining and developing appropriate approaches to conflict transformation and just peace-making in the new globalized context. Therefore, the WCC proclaims the period 2000-2010 as an Ecumenical Decade to Overcome Violence.[9]

Subsequently, the central committee of the WCC has designated "The Ministry of Reconciliation" alongside the emphasis on "Witness and Service amidst Globalization" as one of four overarching themes for the programmatic work of the

WCC in the period up to the next assembly and reaffirmed the decision of the assembly with regard to the Decade to Overcome Violence.[10]

It is the intention and purpose of the following chapters to develop more fully the thinking behind this programmatic concentration on non-violence and reconciliation. This includes a presentation of the aims of the Decade to Overcome Violence. It also requires us to re-examine the question whether a "clash of civilizations" is unavoidable and to what extent the intensification of inter-religious and inter-cultural dialogue is an adequate response to the new configuration of conflicts. A central issue is the question whether intervention, even military intervention if necessary, can be justified as a way to defend human rights and how endangered populations in situations of armed violence can be protected effectively. Finally, the task of building a culture of peace and reconciliation and the reconciling role of the churches in today's world will be addressed. Throughout these reflections the links between the process of globalization and the dramatic increase of conflict and violence will be kept in mind.

2. Overcoming Violence

Ecumenical reflections on a "culture of active non-violence which is life-promoting" (Seoul)[11]

1. With its decision to proclaim the period from 2001 to 2010 as an Ecumenical Decade to Overcome Violence the Harare assembly was responding to a motion in plenary session by the German Mennonite delegate Fernando Enns. The motion and its acceptance by the assembly were obviously inspired by the wide response to the Ecumenical Decade of the Churches in Solidarity with Women (1988-98) which had culminated at the time of the assembly. During the final phase of this decade, the issue of violence against women had caused intense debate. With its decision the assembly was also building on the encouraging experiences with the Programme to Overcome Violence during the preceding years. In the context of this programme, and in particular during the campaign "Peace to the City", a lively process of exchanging experiences and stories had developed about how to stem the increase of violence everywhere and to become agents of reconciliation and peace.

It is the intention of the new decade to build on these positive experiences. In a message sub-titled "Churches Seeking Reconciliation and Peace" announcing the forthcoming decade, the newly elected central committee of the WCC at its first meeting in 1999 affirmed the conviction: "A clear witness to peace and non-violence grounded in justice is what the world needs today from all churches together."[12] However, appeals alone are not sufficient; what is needed is a fundamental change of consciousness.

> We must give up being spectators of violence or merely lamenting it and become active in overcoming violence both within and outside the walls of the church. We remind ourselves and the churches of our common responsibility to speak out boldly against any defence of unjust and oppressive structures, the use of violence and gross violations of human rights committed in the name of any nation or ethnic group.

The search for peace belongs to the centre of the mission of the church.

Leaving behind what separates us, responding ecumenically to the challenge, proving that non-violence is an active approach to conflict resolution, and offering in all humility what Jesus Christ has taught his disciples to do, the churches have a unique message to bring to the violence-ridden world.

The message then points to the many examples which show "that presence in the situations of violence, on the streets and in the war-torn areas, the active involvement with victims and perpetrators of violence" can contribute to transformation and change. In particular, experience gained during the campaign "Peace to the City" has shown that "peace is practical, it grows at grassroots level and is nurtured by the creativity of people". It is the aim of the Decade to provide a forum and to create an ecumenical space where such experiences can be shared; where relationships can be established and processes of learning can be facilitated; where encounter, mutual recognition and encouragement for common action can occur, together also with people of other faith traditions and people of good will.

We will strive together to overcome the spirit, logic and practice of violence. We will work together to be agents of reconciliation and peace with justice in homes, churches and societies as well as in the political, social and economic structures at global level. We will cooperate to build a culture of peace that is based on just and sustainable communities.

At the same meeting in 1999 the central committee also adopted a working document setting out the basic framework for the Decade. This framework document underlines once again that the focus of the Decade is not violence as such, but *overcoming violence*. This is reflected in the proposed methodology, which is to build on positive experiences, by churches, local Christian communities and groups, of overcoming violence. The main objective of the Decade is to move the commitment to peace and to peaceful resolution of conflict away from the margins into the centre of the life and work of the churches. It is recognized that, in this effort, the churches will have to cooperate with each other and with other movements in civil society working for building a culture of peace.

Five areas towards achieving this goal are then identified:

- reaching a comprehensive understanding of the various manifestations of direct as well as structural violence and of the different contextual approaches to overcoming violence;
- relinquishing any theological justification of violence and affirming anew the spirituality of reconciliation and active non-violence;
- creating a new understanding of security in terms of cooperation and community, instead of in terms of domination and competition;
- cooperating with other religious communities in the pursuit of peace and reconciliation and against the misuse of religious and ethnic identities in pluralistic societies;
- challenging the growing militarization of our world, especially the proliferation of small arms and light weapons.

The framework document proposes to structure the Decade in two phases and to envisage an interim evaluation at the time of the ninth assembly of the WCC, which is expected to take place in 2006. It is not the intention of the Decade to initiate detailed scientific and academic analyses of the origins and causes of violence or to formulate comprehensive political and social strategies against violence. Rather it will encourage the churches to engage in focused reflection about violence in view of the challenges of racism, globalization, violence against women, young people and children, etc. The Decade will provide the framework for specific campaigns, like those against land mines or against the proliferation of small arms. A particular emphasis will have to be placed during the Decade on processes of learning and on re-appropriating the traditions of worship and spirituality as resources for the effort to overcome violence. The success of the Decade will depend on whether the churches in their different contexts will respond to this initiative and own it. Experience gained during the previous Decade on

Churches in Solidarity with Women can provide important indications regarding the opportunities and difficulties that lie ahead in the process of giving shape to the Decade.

The Decade was launched internationally during the meeting of the central committee of the WCC at Potsdam, Berlin, in January-February 2001. Many national and regional events have taken place to inaugurate it. Churches and Christian groups in many parts of the world are beginning to develop their own initiatives in response to the Decade call. The international reference group charged with coordinating the Decade process has identified four issues calling for focused reflection during the first phase of the Decade. They are: the anthropological assumptions underlying the culture of violence, the understandings of (1) justice and of (2) power which enter the dynamic of violence, and the response to violence in inter-religious perspective.

2. Violence is a complex phenomenon manifesting itself in many different forms. As indicated above, it is the objective of the Decade to address "holistically the *wide* varieties of *violence,* both direct and structural, in homes, communities, and in international arenas". This holistic approach builds on the insight gained during the ecumenical process on Justice, Peace and the Integrity of Creation that violence is inherent in the underlying dynamic which causes the threats to life. Violence is a basic feature of the ethos of our time. Because of its omnipresence one can even speak of a "culture of violence". The Decade, therefore, focuses not so much on the different, specific manifestations of violence but rather on the common cultural pattern which links them.

This approach, however, provokes the question whether it is not utopian to speak of "overcoming violence". Would it not be more realistic to acknowledge that violence is inherent in human nature and even in creation itself and at best can only be contained and minimized? In addition, would it not be necessary in the context of the Decade to give more specificity to the meaning and use of the very concept of "violence" if the churches are to be encouraged to take a stand against the spreading of the culture of violence?

It is not surprising that there is as yet no common ecumenical response to these questions. Following the inductive methodology proposed by the framework document, no attempt has so far been made to offer a "definition" of violence. Considering the vast variety of languages spoken and used in the churches, this "academic" approach would not be of much value. But even while there is no common definition, the victims of violence know very well what they are exposed to: the direct, physical or emotional disruption of their lives as individuals or communities and the impact of structures which deprive them of the possibility to lead decent lives in dignity. Violence does not only refer to the experience of being impaired in one's bodily integrity; it also affects and destroys the web of relationships sustaining life in community. If indeed the Decade is about overcoming and being liberated from the spirit, logic and practice of violence, then it is of prime importance to gain a better understanding of the dynamic of violence, its hidden assumptions and its sometimes demonic grip or destructive attraction.

Among the issues identified by the international reference group for more in-depth discussion are the explicit or implicit anthropological assumptions underlying the culture of violence. A widely held pessimistic view of human nature would argue that ultimately life is a constant struggle for survival in which only the fittest and strongest will be able to maintain themselves. Ultimately, everyone is left to himself or herself in this struggle and there are only two alternatives: winning or losing. This bipolar, antagonistic reading of the human condition is deeply rooted in Western culture. It leads to an understanding of power as essentially domination of the strong over the weak.

Sometimes these anthropological assumptions are reinforced by biological or scientific arguments pointing to innate aggression as the natural basis for violence. It is even argued that an inclination to violent behaviour may be genetically conditioned. Obviously, for most animals, aggression is instinctively regulated to safeguard the survival of the species. Humans are, however, guided much less by instinct than by social and moral rules and norms learned through a process of cultural socialization. The process of cultural development, in particular the establishment of the rule of law, can be understood as a continuous process of containing the destructive potential of aggression and transforming it into constructive energy.

However, this pessimistic anthropology shapes even the development of cultural regulations for aggressive behaviour. It finds expression in the belief that the threat and even the use of force and violence are indispensable to maintain law and order; and that our efforts to give order to human life are constantly threatened by disorder or chaos, which can ultimately only be contained by violent repression. It is thus violence that guarantees the victory of order over chaos. This conviction is behind the widespread affirmation that peace can only be established through struggle, that security can only be gained through strength.

The French philosopher René Girard in his book *Violence and the Sacred*[13] has undertaken detailed studies of the role which violence plays in the foundational myths of different cultures. In particular, he has given attention to ritual sacrifice and to the symbol of the "scapegoat" as ways in which cultures respond to violence in their midst. The American theologian Walter Wink even speaks of the "myth of redemptive violence". On the basis of his studies in the field of culture and religion, he is convinced that much of human culture is shaped by a sacralization of violence celebrating the victory of order over chaos.

> Life is combat. Any form of order is preferable to chaos, according to this myth. Ours is neither a perfect nor a perfectible world; it is a theater of perpetual conflict in which the prize goes to the strong. Peace through war; security through strength: these are the core convictions that arise from this ancient historical religion, and they form the solid bedrock on which the domination system is founded in every society.[14]

Even if one does not share the views of Girard and Wink, there is enough evidence that this mentality shapes the behaviour of individuals and whole societies. It strongly influenced the period of the cold war and continues to mark the ideology of global capitalism. We encounter vestiges of the same dynamic in the generalized procedures for political decision-making through adversarial debate leading to the victory of the majority over the minority. Even more generally, it is present in the conviction that effective problem-solving involves establishing the clear superiority of one position over any alternatives. This adversarial interpretation of human social relationships has been reinforced strongly by the propagation of competition as the natural condition for economic relationships according to the dynamic of the market.

It is all these hidden or overt assumptions that work together in the dynamic of violence and underlie the "culture of violence". The term culture here refers to attitudes and forms of individual and collective behaviour which accept violence as inevitable and as a natural fact. It is a culture reflecting the process of radical individualization. It encourages people to fight for their "rights" without considering the consequences for the community or their responsibilities towards others. It is a culture in which it is taken for granted that one has to struggle to get what one needs and what one considers to be one's fair share, if need be by using violence.

Efforts to overcome violence have to begin with exploring the basic attitudes of people towards life. The culture of violence draws its energy from a cult of strength and superiority that is often only the cover for a profound disturbance of relationships, for the inability to live in relationships of genuine mutuality. The seeming strength of violence is at the same time its weakness. This was the fundamental insight of Gandhi which led him to develop his concept of "truth power" as the capacity to face up to violence without responding in kind. The courage for non-violent resistance is nourished by a life in mutuality instead of struggle and competition. It understands power as energy for life in commu-

nity which increases as it is being shared. The peaceful resolution of conflicts becomes possible when the win-lose
model is being transformed into a process where both sides
ultimately stand to gain. This is the secret of successful non-
violent struggles: they do not aim at subduing the opponent
but at transforming a relationship of domination into one of
cooperation.

3. It is the goal of the Decade to contribute to overcoming
violence and to the building of a culture of peace. The fore-
going observations on the dynamic of violence and the
anthropological assumptions underlying it indicate that the
decisive first step is to break the spell of violence, to step out
of the cycle by which violence breeds new violence. The
manifestations of violence and the structures supporting the
culture of violence cannot be overcome by counter-violence:
at best they can be contained and limited in their destructive
potential. Any sober and critical analysis of violent revolutions and of violent liberation wars shows that the newly
established structure of governance often does not escape the
dynamic of violence: in many cases it only continues and
reinforces it.

However, breaking the spiral is only the first step. It must
be followed up by efforts to transform the energy of violence
into a source of communication and mutuality. This requires
courage and the power which Gandhi called "truth power".
The experiences with non-violent resistance from Gandhi to
Martin Luther King demonstrate that their seeming power-
lessness in the face of armed structures of power is in fact
their strength: they refuse to bow to violence and thus deny
it the respect and legitimization which it needs for its own
stabilization. The culture of violence follows the logic of
domination and oppression, of victory and defeat. In order to
maintain itself it needs an enemy or a victim, for through the
fear or suffering of the victim the dynamic of violence is
affirmed and renewed. Overcoming violence becomes possible where the intended enemy or victim refuses to accept this
role in a relationship marked by violence. Violence is thus

revealed for what it is: an attitude to life in community which has been distorted and disturbed by non-communication, anxiety, hurt and self-hatred. The perpetrators of violence are thereby included in a relationship of communication and mutuality.

The ethos of non-violence cannot simply be identified with passivity or submission to the manifestations of violence. Rather, it is a form of action that resists violence without using violence itself. This distinction is of fundamental importance for the effort to shape a new consciousness and to build a culture of peace. The affirmations of commitment and the act of covenanting of the world convocation at Seoul (1990), therefore, spoke of "active non-violence" which is "life-affirming". Gandhi's term "truth power" points to the inner strength that manifests itself as the ability to recognize the enemy as a potential partner in a relationship of mutuality and thus to break the spell of violence.

One of the challenges of the Decade to Overcome Violence is to rediscover the biblical roots of the ethos and spirituality of non-violence and peace-making. Walter Wink, in his interpretation of the well-known passages in the Sermon on the Mount (Matt. 5:39-41), insists that non-violence must not be equated with non-resistance.

> The gospel does not teach non-resistance to evil. Jesus counsels resistance, but without violence. The Greek word translated "resist" in Matt. 5:39 is *antistenai*, meaning literally to stand (*stenai*) against (*anti*). What translators have overlooked is that *antistenai* is most often used in the Greek version of the Old Testament as a technical term for warfare. It describes the way opposing armies would march toward each other until their ranks met. Then they would "take a stand", that is, fight... In short, *antistenai* means more here than simply to "resist" evil. It means to resist violently, to revolt or rebel, to engage in an armed insurrection.

All too often, we are told that in the face of violence there are only two alternatives: fight or flight. But Wink concludes:

> Jesus is not telling us to submit to evil, but to refuse to oppose it on its own terms. We are not to let the opponent dictate the

methods of our opposition. He is urging us to transcend both passivity and violence by finding a third way, one that is at once assertive and yet non-violent. The correct translation would be the one still preserved in the earliest renditions of this saying found in the New Testament epistles: "Do not repay evil for evil" (Rom. 12:17; 1 Thess. 5:15; 1 Pet. 3:9). The Scholars Version of Matthew 5:39a is superb: "Don't react violently against the one who is evil."

Wink, therefore, interprets the following examples of the right and the left cheek, of the coat and the cloak, and of the second mile as indications of a behaviour that does not allow the perpetrator of evil or violence to dictate the form or method of reaction.

The logic of Jesus' examples in Matthew 5:39b-41 goes beyond both inaction and overreaction to a new response, fired in the crucible of love, that promises to liberate the oppressed from evil even as it frees the oppressor from sin. Do not react violently to evil, do not counter evil in kind, do not let evil dictate the terms of your opposition, do not let violence lead you to mirror your opponent – this forms the revolutionary principle that Jesus articulates as the basis for non-violently engaging the Powers.

A culture of peace rooted in this ethos of non-violence does not aim at creating a state of complete harmony where all conflicts have ended. Rather, it is characterized by a new consciousness that facilitates a different way of responding even to violent conflicts. This was also the meaning of the call to abolish the institution of war formulated in the context of the process on "Justice, Peace and the Integrity of Creation". The challenge now is to de-legitimize the use of violence and force in responding to conflicts in all areas of life from interpersonal relationships between couples, in the family, in school or at work, to the field of law enforcement by police, the courts or in prison. Non-violent resolution of conflicts in all these areas aims at overcoming the logic of victory and defeat, of winning or losing. A peaceful resolution becomes possible when the relative right and the integrity of both sides in a conflict can be affirmed and thus a broken relationship can be restored. This is expressed in the prophetic saying: "If you remove the yoke from among you, the pointing of the finger, the speaking of evil... (then) you shall be called a repairer of the breach, the restorer of streets to live in" (Isa. 58:9-12).

The attitude and praxis of non-violent action and of peaceful conflict resolution can be learned. And in fact, they presuppose a conscious and critical self-awareness so as not to be caught up in the dynamic of violence and its patterns of reaction. But the ethos of non-violence must not be reduced to a series of techniques and forms of behaviour that can be taught and learned. It is rooted in a spirituality which in the New Testament is described by the terms forgiveness, not insisting on being right, compassion and humility (Col. 3:12f.). Rather than reinforcing the notion that non-violence is an expression of passive submission, humility is that attitude of self-limitation that makes room for the other. Humility, in that sense, is an "ecumenical" virtue, i.e. the deliberate renunciation to insist on one's own right and the readiness to accept others in their difference. It is an expression of the certainty that one's own life and identity are assured and have a foundation beyond the dynamics of power and domination, conflict and competition. Ultimately, the task of overcoming violence calls us to respond to the central command, to love not only our neighbour, but also our enemy. The ability to see in the enemy the person seeking acceptance just as oneself springs from the certainty that one is loved and accepted by God. This is the core of the biblical ethos of non-violence. One of the most penetrating biblical expositions of this ethos is the passage in Romans 12:9-21, which concludes with the sentence: "Do not be overcome by evil, but overcome evil with good" (v.21) and has thus provided the biblical foundation of the Decade to O*vercome* Violence.

4. As indicated in the introduction, the issues of violence and non-violence have been present in ecumenical discussion almost since the beginning a hundred years ago. The present Decade will, however, mark a decisive step going even

beyond the affirmations and commitments made during the conciliar process. Never before has the ecumenical community identified itself so unambiguously with the ethics of non-violence and committed itself to make a culture of peace with justice the central objective of its work. The perspective of the Decade transcends the previous critical responses to violence inspired by "Christian realism" and aimed at minimizing and containing violence. Where violence is seen as the mark of our unredeemed world, the hope that it might be possible to overcome violence will appear as a dangerous illusion. In this sense the pacifist option has always been rejected by the mainline churches in the ecumenical movement, in spite of respect for the ethical integrity of its defenders. So far, the "privileged option for non-violence" has remained a minority position in the ecumenical movement, represented by the historic peace churches as well as small groups in the mainline Protestant churches who accept the commitment for Christian peace service. With this Decade the ecumenical community has accepted the ambitious goal to move the option for a culture of peace from the margins into the centre of the life and witness of the churches. This conscious decision in favour of a period of ten years reflects the insight that what is called for is a long-term process of change of consciousness and not only a time-limited programme of study and action.

Considering Christian history and its many manifestations of involvement with structures and processes of violence, there might be good reason to doubt whether the churches in the ecumenical community will be capable of that change of mentality and consciousness which would enable them to become agents of a culture of reconciliation and peace. The message of the central committee expresses the readiness for critical self-assessment:

> We are also aware that Christians and churches have added, through words and actions, to growing violence and injustice in a world of oppression and graceless competition. We are yearning for a community of humankind, in which nobody is excluded and everybody can live in peace with human dignity.

> We want to engage in constructive efforts to build a culture of peace. But we know this requires from us a deep process of change, which starts with repentance and a renewed commitment to the very sources of our faith.[15]

Even though it is the primary goal of the Decade to encourage the churches to undertake concrete steps towards overcoming violence and peaceful conflict resolution, it will also have to lead the churches to review and question critically those traditions of teaching and praxis which in the past have justified and legitimated structures of violence and still do. Among these are "violent" images of God and interpretations of the atonement, but also hierarchical structures of power and a spirituality of obedience, submission to authority and self-abasement, and finally an understanding of mission in terms of a "crusade". Many of these issues have been addressed in feminist theology under the heading of "patriarchy" and the male-centred mentality that has shaped much of Christian theological tradition. In the context of the Decade, this discussion will have to be re-opened and continued.

Thus, the Decade can and should lead to efforts to re-appropriate earlier insights gained in ecumenical discussion. This is true, in particular, for the intensive debate about violence against women, even in the church; for experiences of violence in the context of racial and ethnic discrimination; for the many approaches to an intentional education for peace; and for the more recent initiatives and campaigns against anti-personnel land mines and the proliferation of small arms. Mention should be made as well of the worldwide network which has developed in relation to the campaign "Peace to the City" and which could become a crystallizing focus for the Decade.

Against the background of confrontations between religious communities, e.g. in Indonesia, in the Sudan, and in Nigeria, where the religious loyalties of Muslims and Christians are being used to fuel conflict, particular attention will have to be given to inter-religious dialogue as an important element in efforts to build a culture of peace. As has been pointed out before, economic injustice and the widening of the gap between rich and poor as a consequence of global capitalism have to be counted among the main causes of conflict; some have even begun to talk about "economically instituted violence". Therefore, the Decade will have to be linked closely with the efforts to create a more just and sustainable order in the global economy.

Of course, the Decade cannot claim to deal systematically with all manifestations of violence. Its primary objective is to establish the ethical, spiritual and practical credibility of the commitment to *overcome* violence and to work out the implications of this alternative logic through the exchange and linkage of concrete experiences. The Decade itself is meant as a "symbolic space" in which mutual encouragement and critical questioning can take place, where conflicts can be addressed and dissenting voices be heard. Its intention is to facilitate the forming of alliances with other partners in the context of civil society who are also committed to the building of a culture of peace. The parallelism between the Decade and the simultaneous UN Decade for a Culture of Peace and Non-Violence for the Children of the World opens opportunities for cooperation that will have to be utilized. The same is true for cooperation with other religious communities and groups in the common resistance against the exploitation of religious differences in the interest of power struggles and strategies of violence.

The Decade provides a framework for continuing and intensifying ecumenical discussion on the foundations of a Christian ethic of peace and for developing new forms of active Christian peace service in conflict situations. An encouraging recent example is the establishment of an "Ecumenical Monitoring Programme for Peace in Israel and Palestine", in which local churches and the regional ecumenical organization cooperate with overseas churches and ecumenical agencies under the umbrella of the WCC.

One of the insights gained during the conciliar process on "Justice, Peace and the Integrity of Creation" was the conviction that the traditional doctrine of a "just war", which had been at the centre of Christian peace ethic for centuries, had to be replaced by the concept of a "just peace". This insight has to be developed and tested more intentionally. The shift would imply that the ethical question should no longer be under what conditions the use of armed force could be considered an act of justice, but rather what are the basic requirements of justice that must be met in order to speak of a just and durable peace. In further discussion about the ethics of peace this approach would have to be applied to the different dimensions of the work for peace and security as they have been identified in the "Agenda for Peace" of the United Nations (1992), i.e. preventive diplomacy, peace-making, peace-keeping, and post-conflict peace-building. It might then become apparent that the churches, because of their presence among the smallest units of human community, have unique opportunities to repair and restore the threatened networks of social relationships, to overcome enemy images, and to strengthen people in their resolve to resist the spreading of a culture of violence. It is realized today that measures of preventive conflict resolution and the creation of early warning systems are particularly important. The churches are in a position to discern the development of conflicts even before they have become confrontational. They can, therefore, make a contribution to the timely discernment of civil and interstate conflicts and thus prepare the way for preventive initiatives.

The Decade should identify ways how churches in conflict situations can become advocates of truth and of unimpeded communication. There are many examples from recent years showing that the churches and ecumenical organizations can play an important role by providing both sides in a conflict situation with accurate information, by exposing propaganda and false information and thus preparing the ground for resuming contact and communication. Reference could also be made to the model of round tables which played a significant role in the "autumn revolution" in Central and Eastern Europe and which was essentially inspired by a Christian ethos of peaceful conflict resolution. It has meanwhile been adopted as a framework for negotiation within the ecumenical community itself in situations where conflicting interests have to be reconciled. In any case, the churches can draw on the long tradition of conciliar conflict resolution which should be brought to bear again today, not only on the internal life of the churches but also on social and political conflicts.

For many, the conciliar process and in particular the large ecumenical assemblies in 1989 and 1990 raised expectations that the churches would be able together to make an authoritative witness for justice, peace and the integrity of creation, a witness "that the world will have to hear" (D. Bonhoeffer). The approach of the Decade is both more humble and more ambitious at the same time: the Decade places its hopes not so much in the critical-prophetic act of confessing, but rather in the process of learning and entering into the spirituality and praxis of active non-violence. The churches have realized, not least in the course of the conciliar process and the Decade of the Churches in Solidarity with Women, that they are themselves part of the problem. They cannot expect that in ten years' time, at the end of the Decade, violence will have been overcome; but they trust that the spirit of reconciliation will transform them and enable them to become instruments of a culture of peace for all people.

3. Is the "Clash of Civilizations" Unavoidable?[16]

The ecumenical Decade to Overcome Violence in the context of the debate about globalization

1. In the summer of 1993 the American political scientist Samuel Huntington published an article in the journal *Foreign Affairs* under the title "The Clash of Civilizations". In his article, which provoked an unusually broad discussion, Huntington presented an initial analysis of issues of global security and of the specific national interests of the United States after the end of the cold war. Three years later, Huntington published a book on the same topic under the title.[17] The debate on the theses formulated by Huntington has continued in recent years, not without some passion. Obviously, it is of immediate significance for the ecumenical project of a decade to overcome violence.

Meanwhile, the general assembly of the United Nations decided on 4 November 1998 to proclaim the year 2001 as a year of the United Nations for a "Dialogue among Civilizations". The decision was prompted by a proposal by the Iranian state president Khatami that had received the support of the Conference of Islamic States; it is intended as an explicit response to the prognosis by Huntington. It also fits into a conscious emphasis in the work of the United Nations, which had already begun with the International Year of Tolerance in 1995 and was continued in 2000 with an International Year for a Culture of Peace. In addition, the decision prepared the ground for the projected International Decade for a Culture of Peace and Non-Violence for the Children of the World, which was clearly in the mind of the Harare assembly of the WCC when it initiated the Ecumenical Decade to Overcome Violence.

Further, Pope John Paul II entitled his traditional peace message for the year 2001 "Dialogue between Cultures for a Civilization of Love and Peace". Recognizing that the process of globalization has given rise to movements of resistance defending cultural identities, the pope addressed the fear that we might be moving towards a clash of civilizations struggling for power and domination

The question, therefore, has to be addressed: Is a clash of civilizations unavoidable and what could the implications be for the Decade to Overcome Violence, its objectives and its methodology? Both questions are obviously related to the controversial debate about the interpretation and the assessment of the effects of globalization. This is also the starting point of Huntington. Contrary to the widespread assumption that the process of modernization and the worldwide extension of Western, consumerist values will lead to a homogenized global culture, Huntington attempts to show that modernization and Westernization are not simultaneous and one-directional processes. He is convinced that the predominance of the West will decrease over the coming decades and that we are already seeing a revival of traditional values, particularly in the Islamic countries and in Asia, which can exist alongside efforts at modernization. Huntington sees the world after the historic changes in the 1990s as a polycentric configuration of nine major civilizations, the relationships between which include a great potential for conflict. As a political realist he ventures the prognosis that the conflicts inherent in the clash of civilizations will take the place of the former confrontation of ideological blocks.

If this analysis is valid, then the question has to be asked how these potential and even actual conflicts can be managed. It is of course Huntington's concern to prepare the countries of the West and, in particular, the United States as the leading economic and military power of the West for this new configuration of a polycentric and multi-cultural world. But he does not consider a "clash" in the sense of a violent confrontation as unavoidable.

Huntington's analysis has drawn widespread critical responses based on empirical and historical arguments. In particular, it is argued that his ideal-typical distinction of large cultural blocks with an inherent tendency to uniformity neglects and underestimates the dynamic of cultural interpenetration leading to the emergence of hybrid cultures. However, it is not easy to refute his conclusion that we are moving towards a multicultural world where it is unlikely or impossible that one single culture will reign supreme. As a consequence he considers the conscious recognition of the multicultural global situation as a fundamental condition for global security. He believes that the different civilizations share sufficient common values so as to make communication between them possible. This leads him to argue at the end of his book for the building of an international order on the basis of recognition of these large civilizations as the best protection against another world war. However, his whole analysis is directed so much towards considering potential conflict scenarios, including military confrontation, that his concluding plea gives the impression of a belated response to some of his critics.

2. It corresponds to this perspective that the initiatives on the level of the United Nations are oriented towards searching for commonalities between cultures and civilizations, i.e. for elements that could facilitate dialogue and mutual exchange and could serve effectively to counteract the dangerous scenario of a "clash of civilizations". The advocates of these initiatives refer to the emergence of a "new paradigm" according to which cultural differences and diversity are no longer considered as a threat but rather as an opportunity for common growth and mutual enrichment. The basic concept of the United Nations implies the recognition of these differences. Growing worldwide integration and the development of a stock of common values do not exclude the preservation of distinct cultural identities. Genuine dialogue is based on the recognition of these different cultures; it aims at mutual understanding and works against the tendency to interpret otherness and difference as a threat and thus as a justification for a militant defence and protection of particular identities. Furthering dialogue between cultures and civilizations thus becomes an important element in all political efforts towards peace and security in this period after the end of the cold war under the conditions of globalization.

This comprehensive and somewhat ambitious perspective, however, does not easily lend itself to being translated into a programme of action. The implications of globalization in the area of cultures are far from clear and the appeal for a positive appreciation of cultural diversity and of the global multicultural situation runs the risk of taking the real conflicts too lightly. But it is certainly important for the thinking behind the Ecumenical Decade to Overcome Violence – in parallel with the corresponding UN Decade – to take note of the fact that the increased dynamic of the process of globalization after the end of the cold war has been accompanied by a growing potential for conflict. Some would even talk of the emergence of a "culture of violence".

The inter-relationship between these two processes would need further detailed analysis, not least against the background of Huntington's theses. Even so, there is no question that economic globalization is being experienced by many of those who are among the "losers" as a force which violently disrupts social and cultural structures by marginalizing and excluding those who have no opportunity to participate in market competition. The pressures of deregulation and privatization which expose more and more segments of the life of societies to the logic of the market is provoking increasing resistance. Globalization has to be seen as one of the causes of the revitalization and active defence of ethnic, national, cultural and religious identities. The various forms of militant religious-political fundamentalism can be understood as a manifestation of this resistance against globalization, even though they might in some respects go along with modernization. Another form of this resistance is the attempt among minorities or larger groups of migrants and immigrants to reconstruct their national and ethnic identities. All of this is being reinforced by a process of religious resurgence, particularly in countries which have not followed the Western, secular differentiation between religion and general culture. The most obvious example of this is the so-called "Islamism", i.e. the effort to revive a comprehensive Islamic culture in opposition to what is being perceived as "Western" culture and civilization. In addition, in the context of globalization all cultures are experiencing growing religious and cultural plurality, which may be seen as a threat by those who want to maintain the dominance of their traditional cultural and religious world-view.

3. The increase of cultural plurality, both within countries and worldwide, was also the starting point for Huntington's analysis. Since he understands civilization as an integrated and self-contained ensemble of structures, attitudes and values, he sees plurality in the first instance as a source of potential conflicts. While he pleads for the recognition of cultural plurality on the global level as a protection against destructive conflicts, he does not consider that genuine cultural plurality is viable and sustainable within each of the large civilization blocks that he has identified. Leaving aside the critical discussion of many of his detailed arguments, his studies have served to underline the conflictual character of a globalized world. The conflicts have been steadily increasing and they seem to be linked directly with the process of globalization. What is much less clear, however, is the question whether these conflicts will manifest themselves along the cultural and civilizational fault-lines, as Huntington suggests. It is far more likely that they will arise around struggles for power and influence, access to natural and energy resources, water and arable land. They can lead to violent confrontations, but this is certainly not inevitable. In many instances, such conflicts are being fuelled by financial resources originating from the global shadow economy of the arms trade, drug-trafficking or commerce in precious materials like diamonds. In a situation where national borders do not constitute a barrier any more, governmental and intergovernmental authorities have lost most of the instruments of control. In any case, in most of recent civil conflicts ethnic, cultural and religious differences and tensions have not been the primary source of confrontation. Rather, they have been used deliberately in the interest of mobilizing the support of the population for a confrontational scenario. Huntington employs a static and largely unhistorical concept of culture or civilization that leads him to focus one-sidedly

on cultural-religious differences and tensions as the primary causes of potential conflicts.

Nevertheless, the fact remains that the growing cultural and religious plurality is unstable and fragile. It includes a high potential for conflict, both within and between societies and cultural groups. This gives added urgency to efforts aimed at giving an intentional shape to the relationships between cultural and religious traditions. All attempts to contain and minimize the potential of conflict and violence in the globalized world will remain ineffective or futile as long as they concentrate their attention only on the symptoms and their control. The experience gathered during the long period of trying to build a viable international order still remains valid under the conditions of globalization, namely that effective security can never be based solely on containment of a potential adversary. Durable security presupposes that the legitimate security interests of both sides are recognized and that the potential adversaries, therefore, are obliged to cooperate.

The effort to "overcome" or at least to contain violence in the context of local communities as well as within or between societies must, therefore, be guided by an alternative consciousness, a new "paradigm" or "culture" able to respond to the challenges of globalization and its impact on the lives of people. If it is true that globalization is not leading to an inescapable cultural uniformity but will sharpen the situation of plurality and thus the potential of conflict, this has significant implications for the project to overcome violence. It will have to place priority emphasis on efforts to develop locally and globally a culture of dialogue and communication. In that sense the call by the United Nations for a year of the "dialogue of civilizations" is a step in the right direction. It builds on many initiatives in the field of inter-religious encounter like the declaration on a "global ethic" by the Parliament of the World's Religions meeting in Chicago 1993. The declaration is based on the studies by Hans Küng on the common moral and ethical orientations shared by the great religions which could, therefore, serve as a framework of binding norms and values for a globalized world. In the context of preparations for the millennium assembly of the United Nations other similar initiatives were undertaken like the Millennium World Peace Summit of Religious and Spiritual Leaders held in New York in August 2000 with its solemn declaration on peace, or the formulation of an "Earth Charter" which was presented publicly in June 2000.

Obviously, the development of a "culture of dialogue" will only be successful if the necessary space is provided to work out and test commonly accepted rules which can regulate the relationships between different partners, whether societies, cultures or religions. Affirming a culture of dialogue does not involve disregarding or denying the existence of tensions or the potential for conflict between different collective identities. It is the purpose of dialogue to transform a situation of defensive perceptions of each other into one of constructive mutuality and thus to help the partners to enlarge their own identity. Working for a "culture" of dialogue, or of peace and non-violence, also means working for the transformation of those integrated understandings of culture which often involve having a strong sense of one's own distinctive identity over against the "other". This is the weakness of Huntington's concept of civilization.[18]

The Decade to Overcome Violence seeks to tie in with the efforts to build such a new culture of dialogue, of peace and non-violence by highlighting the concrete and constructive local forms of resistance against the spread of the culture of violence. Cultures are not built and developed systematically as integral systems. They emerge through communicative processes and are engaged in constant transformation. This is true not only for the revitalization and defence of "traditional" cultural identities over against the pressures of globalization. We are witnessing simultaneously the development of new cultural patterns and attitudes which arise and gain acceptance in specific local contexts and are then shared in networks of intercultural communication. The primary interest of the ecumenical decade is not to shape a new global system of values or a global ethic. It seeks rather to transform the potential of conflict in the encounter between different cultural identities into constructive energy.

The "clash of civilizations" is not unavoidable. The Ecumenical Decade to Overcome Violence together with the corresponding UN Decade point to the need to transform the potentially conflictual situation of plurality in a globalized world in the direction of a genuine culture of dialogue and mutuality. Solemn declarations and conferences of the United Nations can sharpen the awareness for the task ahead. The alternative culture responding to the challenges of globalization will be built, however, through processes of networking and interaction between people in their respective life contexts. This is the area where the ecumenical decade can make a real difference.

4. Human Rights: Foundation for a Culture of Peace[19]

1. The ecumenical commitment to peace and reconciliation has always been guided by the conviction that durable peace and genuine reconciliation must be rooted in the realization of justice. It has become increasingly clear that respect for human rights and their implementation have to be considered a fundamental condition for achieving social justice. Disregard for human rights in many cases is linked with direct or structural violence and in turn often gives rise to violent forms of reaction. Overcoming violence and advocacy on behalf of human rights should therefore be seen as closely interrelated and should reinforce each other. Since its beginnings the ecumenical movement has promoted the development of an international legal order and the universal recognition of human rights as vitally important elements for the peaceful and non-violent resolution of conflicts.

More recently, the Harare assembly of the WCC reaffirmed the intimate connection between the defence of human rights and the search for non-violent forms of conflict resolution. The paragraph on "non-violence and reconciliation" in the report of the Programme Guidelines Committee, already quoted above, says:

> Truth, justice and peace together represent values basic to granting of human rights, inclusion and reconciliation. When these values are ignored, trust is replaced by fear and human power no longer serves the gift of life and the sanctity and dignity of all in creation. Violence arising from various forms of human-rights violations, discrimination and structural injustice represents a growing concern at all levels of an increasingly plural society. Racism combines with and aggravates other causes of exclusion and marginalization. Conflicts are becoming increasingly complex, located more often within nations than between nations. Women and children in conflict situations represent a special concern. There is a need to bring together the work on gender and racism, human rights and transformation of conflict in ways that engage the churches in initiatives for reconciliation that build on repentance, truth, justice, reparation and forgiveness.[20]

This paragraph concludes with the proclamation of the Ecumenical Decade to Overcome Violence.

In the context of the Ecumenical Decade special and renewed attention will have to be given to the role of human rights instruments in efforts to build a culture of peace. Human rights define limits to the exercise of legitimate power and where these limits are disregarded, power turns into violence. Conversely, the progressive development of human rights instruments and their application as cornerstones for an international legal order have to be considered as decisive steps in any effort to overcome structures of violence and to build a culture of peace.

Ecumenical discussion has always given special attention to the concern for human rights. Initially, the interest was focused on making sure that the right to religious liberty was included in the broader framework of human rights. This corresponded to the traditional understanding of human rights which aimed in the first instance at protecting individual liberties. The widening of the concept of human rights through the two international covenants of 1966 on "civil and political" as well as on "social, economic and cultural" rights prompted a reassessment and a reformulation of the ecumenical approach to human rights issues. The comprehensive declaration on human rights of the Nairobi assembly of the WCC (1975) placed the concern for human rights into the context of the struggles for liberation from poverty, colonialism, institutionalized racism and military dictatorship. As a consequence, the defence of human rights became a yardstick for the achievement of social justice.

In the period following the Nairobi assembly the ecumenical movement became increasingly involved in efforts to sharpen human rights standards through the development of international conventions for the affirmation and defence of the rights of the child, of women, indigenous people, minorities and uprooted people; for protection against discrimination, racial violence and torture; against violence against women, including rape as a weapon of war; against extra-judicial executions and the death penalty. All these initiatives were aimed at sharpening the concept of human rights and the use of the instruments for their effective implementation. They also helped us to gain a deeper understanding of human rights as foundational for a culture of peace and a peaceful, non-violent resolution of conflicts.

2. The Harare assembly of the WCC not only proclaimed the Ecumenical Decade to Overcome Violence. Building on a comprehensive review process of the concept of human rights and the corresponding praxis among the churches in the ecumenical movement, the assembly adopted a detailed policy statement on human rights. The statement begins by addressing the new challenges which human-rights work is facing as a consequence of globalization and the tendency to politicize the human rights discourse. In response to the danger of weakening and eroding official recognition of human-rights norms, the statement reaffirms the basic ecumenical conviction that human rights are indivisible and have universal validity. It formulates ecumenical positions regarding the current international debates about the abolition of the death penalty, the rights of women, of indigenous and uprooted people, and of people with disabilities. Even though the statement does not link its defence of human rights in these specific cases with the aim of overcoming violence, it is obvious that it points here, at least implicitly, to widespread manifestations of direct or structural violence.

Of particular relevance in this present context is the paragraph dealing with "human rights and peace-making". The statement says:

> Human rights are the essential basis for a just and durable peace. Failure to respect them often leads to conflict and warfare, and several times during this century it has led to genocide as a result of uncontrolled ethnic, racial or religious hatred. The international community has time and again shown itself incapable of stopping genocide once it has begun. There is an urgent need to learn the lessons of the past, and to set up mechanisms of early intervention when the danger signs appear. The churches are often most well placed to see the impending danger...

The paragraph then refers to the importance of devoting explicit attention to human rights standards in connection with efforts aimed at the prevention or resolution of conflicts, e.g. in the context of UN peace missions. It is thus important that the legal structures for the protection of human rights be reinstated after an acute conflict has ended and that any peace accord explicitly reaffirms the basic international human rights norms.

In this connection, the statement also addresses the urgent problem of impunity for violations of human rights. It states:

> An essential part of post-conflict healing is the pursuit of truth, justice for victims, forgiveness and reconciliation in societies which have suffered systematic violations of human rights. We support the efforts of churches and human rights groups in such societies in their struggle to overcome impunity for past crimes whose authors have been given official protection from prosecution. Impunity perpetuates injustice, which in turn generates acts of revenge and endless violence, to the extent of genocide, as we have experienced on different occasions throughout this century.

The prevention of impunity in the case of massive violations of human rights has therefore to be considered as an important contribution to efforts to re-establish peaceful order in society. Along the same lines the declaration welcomes explicitly the agreement to establish an International Criminal Court, which should help the international community in its enforcement of human rights.

It is important to hold those responsible for violations of human rights accountable for their actions and thus to grant justice to the victims, including measures of restitution and reparation. However, such endeavours alone are not sufficient to establish a durable order of peace in society. The deliberate efforts to face the legacy of the apartheid conflict in South Africa and of the massive violations of human rights committed during that period have shown that an understanding of justice focusing on retribution can itself become the source of new violence. The enforcement of human rights must be guided by an understanding of justice as "restorative justice" if it is to contribute to peace and reconciliation in society.

3. Under normal circumstances the aims of overcoming violence and enforcing human rights complement and reinforce each other. However, there are situations where they can enter into tension and conflict. Thus, while it is perfectly legitimate for a particular ethnic, national or social group to struggle for the recognition of their rights, such campaigning can endanger the coherence of a given society and become the cause of violence. The ecumenical movement has become deeply involved in acts of resistance against the many manifestations of structural violence in the form of racial discrimination and oppression, economic exploitation, and ideological or political dictatorship. This has led to repeated debates about the question whether and under what circumstances the use of counter-violence can be considered a legitimate means of defending and enforcing elementary human rights. However, the experiences in connection with violent revolutions and liberation wars show that even so-called "counter-violence" as a rule does not escape the logic of violence. A successful violent revolution does not create a sufficient basis of legitimacy for a new framework of governance and power. In spite of its sympathy and its understanding for the conditions which have led anti-colonial liberation movements to move to a strategy of armed resistance, after long periods of non-violent struggle, as for example in South Africa, the ecumenical movement has consistently refrained from acknowledging counter-violence as a legitimate means of "last resort". It has limited itself to the position of not passing judgment on those who feel constrained to use violence in the struggle for their rights.

This controversial debate, which was carried on particularly in the context of the struggle against racism, is now entering a new phase as the ecumenical movement engages in the Decade to Overcome Violence. In fact, the possibility of tension between the commitment to peace and non-violence and for resistance against massive violations of human rights has been brought into sharp focus by the more recent conflicts in the Balkans and in Africa. This has led to intense debate about the legitimacy of so-called "humanitarian intervention", i.e. whether and how populations which are endangered through situations of armed conflict and the related violations of human rights can be protected effectively, and, especially, whether the use of military force can be considered a legitimate means to remove the danger and re-establish an order of peace and respect for human rights.

In this regard, the international community is facing an ethical and legal-political dilemma. Until the middle of the 20th century it was considered as legitimate under customary international law for states to intervene in the internal affairs of other states in cases where their own citizens were exposed to threats of life and security or where the other state massively violated the elementary rights of its own citizens. Under the impression that international order had been eroded as a consequence of two world wars, the international conference in San Francisco 1945 included in the charter of the United Nations the principle of non-intervention in the internal affairs of a sovereign state (art. 2.7). The charter aims at an order of peace that gives absolute priority to peaceful means of resolving conflict. This is expressed in the prohibition to resort to the threat or the use of force in relationships between sovereign states (art 2.4), with the exception of a case of individual or collective self-defence (art. 51.) The provisions of chapter VII also allow the use of force under conditions set by the Security Council of the United Nation with the aim of restoring international peace and security. There have been a number of instances in the past where the Security Council has authorized military intervention to respond to a serious breach of international peace and security. However, the charter does not recognize a right to intervene on "humanitarian" grounds. As a basic rule, the members of the United Nations are obliged to respect one another's sovereignty and settle all disputes peacefully, eventually by taking a conflict to the International Court of Justice.

At the same time, however, the charter of the United Nations affirms the universal validity of human rights and member states are constrained under the charter to further and strengthen respect for and the implementation of human rights and basic freedoms for all people, irrespective of race, gender, language or religion (art. 1.3). The charter also recognizes that "universal respect for, and observance of, human rights and fundamental freedoms for all" is essential for international peace (art. 55c). This implies that the United Nations cannot disregard situations of massive human-rights violations in any one of its member states. This responsibility is entrusted to the Commission on Human Rights and to the recently created office of High Commissioner for Human Rights. Like other activities of the United Nations grouped under the authority of the Economic and Social Council, these special human rights organs lack the ability to enforce their decisions effectively. In addition, situations of extreme humanitarian emergency, including civil war or the threat of starvation of a whole population, which constitute a violation of basic human rights, have so far not been included in the agenda of the Human Rights Commission. In cases, therefore, where a government is unable or unwilling in view of internal conflicts to protect the basic human rights of its citizens, the international community finds itself in the dilemma that the charter prevents direct intervention for the protection of the population while at the same time obliging the members to work for the implementation of human rights for all everywhere. The same tension arose in the discussion about the implementation of the final act of the Conference for Security and Cooperation in Europe with regard to the implications of principles VI and VII, calling for respect of sovereignty and non-interference in internal affairs and the respect for human rights respectively.

In most instances, however, this dilemma of conflicting principles can be resolved when it is recognized that the charter of the United Nations does provide in chapter 6 for a wide range of possibilities to apply diplomatic pressure, to impose economic or other sanctions, or to intervene through the deployment of peace-keeping forces below the level of using force in order to prevent a conflictual situation from turning into open confrontation or to resolve an armed conflict after it has broken out. In line with the spirit of the charter the ecumenical movement has given priority attention to such measures of conflict prevention and of non-violent response to armed conflict. This applies also to instances of conflict prompted by human rights violations, and the Human Rights Commission has developed its own instruments, like the appointment of special rapporteurs, the sending of fact finding or observer missions, or the inclusion of human rights observers in peace missions of the United Nations. Since elections have increasingly become occasions for violent confrontation and for infringement of human rights, the churches in the ecumenical movement have become actively involved in setting up programmes for election monitoring.

4. The conflicts in Rwanda and in the former Yugoslavia have, however, produced humanitarian crises and violations of human rights of such magnitude that all the available possibilities of response and intervention below the level of force seemed to remain ineffective and the call for an armed intervention on "humanitarian grounds" became very strong, even among churches in the ecumenical movement. In each of the specific cases it can be argued that a timely and consistent use of non-military forms of pressure and intervention could have prevented the resulting catastrophe of genocide in the case of Rwanda and of "ethnic cleansing" in the case of Bosnia-Herzegovina and Kosovo. And yet, as and when the humanitarian crises were developing, armed intervention seemed to be the "last resort".

It should be noted that in neither case did the Security Council of the United Nations authorize an intervention on the basis of article 39 of the charter by invoking a breach of international peace and security. The NATO interventions in Yugoslavia, therefore, were not covered formally by international law. Even so, the dilemma was recognized on the level of the United Nations and led to a thorough review of the United Nations Peace Operations (Brahimi report). In his address to the UN general assembly in September 1999 the secretary general underlined this legal and moral-ethical dilemma in the following terms:

> To those for whom the greatest threat to the future of international order is the use of force in the absence of a Security Council mandate, one might ask – not in the case of Kosovo – but in the context of Rwanda: If, in those dark days and hours leading up to the genocide, a coalition of states had been prepared to act in defence of the Tutsi population, but did not receive prompt Council authorization, should such a coalition have stood aside and allowed the horror to unfold?
>
> To those for whom the Kosovo action heralded a new era when states and groups of states can take military action outside the established mechanism for enforcing international law, one might ask: Is there not a danger of such interventions undermining the imperfect, yet resilient, security system created after the second world war, and of setting dangerous precedents for future interventions without a clear criterion to decide who might invoke these precedents, and in what circumstances?[21]

In particular the NATO intervention in Kosovo, which was officially justified on "humanitarian" grounds, has sharpened the dilemma. A military intervention causing disproportionate numbers of civilian casualties and vast damage to the civilian infrastructure in violation of the Geneva convention cannot be considered "humanitarian". Further, it distorts the accepted understanding of the criteria for humanitarian action, i.e. universality, independence, impartiality, and humanity. Humanitarian action, e.g. by the International Red Cross or other voluntary agencies, aims at assistance or protection irrespective of religion, ethnic or national origin, and political or religious conviction. These humanitarian ideals have to be protected against being confused with military considerations. Human rights, in particular, cannot be enforced by military means. In contrast to military logic, it is precisely the purpose of international humanitarian law to protect the rights and dignity of people in situations of war.

5. The dilemma of how to resolve the tension between the commitment to peace and non-violence and the requirement to protect people in situations of massive human-rights violations has manifested itself also in ecumenical discussion. No conclusive response has so far been found. At its last meeting in January-February 2001, while launching the Decade to Overcome Violence, the central committee of the WCC also considered a background document on "The Protection of Endangered Populations in Situations of Armed Violence: Towards an Ecumenical Ethical Approach".[22] The document begins by reviewing the ecumenical discussion on the issues involved and recalls in particular the controversial debates in reaction to the conflicts in Somalia, Bosnia, Rwanda and Kosovo. As a first result of a critical analysis, which also took account of the report reviewing the UN Peace Operations, the document proposes avoiding the term "humanitarian intervention" because it gives rise to confusing and misleading interpretations. Instead it suggests that we should speak (as in its title) of the "protection of endangered populations in situations of armed violence".

The document reaffirms the basic ecumenical conviction that conflict prevention must have absolute priority over against the eventual use of military force. Even if prevention fails, there exist (as pointed out above) a number of non-violent ways of responding to conflict, including in particular the instruments of the human rights organs of the United Nations, like the sending of fact finding or investigation commissions or the appointment of special rapporteurs. The document also underlines the fact that article 41 of the charter of the United Nations provides for the possibility of imposing sanctions, which were the subject of a special memorandum presented to the central committee in 1995. At that time, however, the central committee recognized that sanctions also constitute a form of "violent" interference. Frequently they hurt the civilian population more directly than those responsible for a conflict or humanitarian crisis. They are, moreover, seldom applied consistently and thus lose their effectiveness.

The document then addresses specifically the tension between the principle of national sovereignty and of non-interference and the obligation to respect and protect human rights. The international convention against genocide of 1948 is the only instance where the international community has accepted the legitimacy and even the obligation to disregard the sovereignty of a given state in order to prevent a crime against humanity. This raises the question whether situations where the relevant government authority is unable or unwilling to prevent systematic, continuous and massive human rights violations can be considered as fulfilling the conditions for intervention under the convention against genocide. So far, there is no consensus among those responsible for international law or policy making.

The document strongly argues against any unilateral action and says:

> Whenever aggression or massive and flagrant abuses of human rights by one nation call for preventive or punitive action under international law, a concerted multilateral response authorized by the United Nations or other competent international body is most likely to meet the requirements of just peace-making.

But then it continues:

> Recent international military engagements undertaken in some situations in the name of "humanitarian intervention" and the failure to intervene in others have raised serious moral and ethical questions. How can the international community come to the aid of people in crisis in a proportionate and consistent manner which gives equal value to all life?

As a provisional conclusion the document states

> that it is ever necessary to consider the use of armed force in international relations is a reflection of the failure of the international community to have responded in a timely and appropriate fashion to prevent a conflict or to resolve a conflict during its early stages. An inadequate or inconsistent response to human suffering compounds the moral failure. Recent decisions to intervene with massive armed force have often been influenced by globalized public media that tend to report in a selec-

tive way, exaggerating some and ignoring others where equal or greater numbers of people were at imminent risk.

Christians are called to a ministry of just peace-making. But they cannot escape making decisions involving moral and ethical uncertainties. Thus,

the question arises whether, from an ecumenical Christian perspective, the international community should refrain from taking up arms even to protect endangered populations in situations of armed violence or to defend those deployed by competent international authority for this purpose. Here competing moral and ethical values must be considered. Some Christians say yes, believing that the teachings of Jesus require us to oppose any use of armed force. Others say no, considering that the protection of human life may require it to do so in extreme situations, and recognizing that any such decision should be approached with great humility. In either case, responsibility for unintended consequences must be accepted both by those who choose to use armed force and by those who do not.

The moral and ethical dilemma regarding the use of force as a "last resort" with the purpose of defending human rights will continue to be discussed controversially during the Decade to Overcome Violence. In an appendix the document develops a series of considerations and criteria as a possible guide to decision-making. Here a clear distinction is made between general violations of human rights and those cases where one would have to speak of "crimes against humanity". The criteria also emphasize the need to differentiate strictly between military actions aimed at the protection of endangered people or populations and military actions in the case of war. In the first case, it is more appropriate to think of the model of police intervention in the interest of protecting the population and of maintaining public order.

However one might evaluate the formulation of such criteria, their appropriateness and possible further refinement – the central committee was not unanimous in its response – it is clear that this discussion has been placed into a new framework with the Decade to Overcome Violence. Now, the primary concern is no longer how to respond to violence in the form of human-rights violations, but rather how a culture of peace can be built in which the universal validity and indivisibility of human rights is recognized. To fight human-rights violations is necessary, but it is not an end in itself. It points beyond the defensive position of containing violence towards the vision of a world without violence. This vision is rooted in the certainty of faith that the gospel of Jesus Christ is a power that can change and transform our world marked by violence. It is not a political project to be judged on the basis of its feasibility and effectiveness. Rather, it sets us free from the constraints of "real-politik" and thus releases the energies needed for building a culture of peace. This is both the challenge and the opportunity of the Decade to Overcome Violence.

5. Reconciliation: A Challenge to the Churches[23]

1. Our world is full of conflict and violence: between states and communities, in cities and on the streets, in schools and homes. The images of innocent victims and the names of the places of their suffering come in such rapid succession that our capacity to comprehend and our ability to respond are being paralyzed. To speak of reconciliation in this context is both urgently necessary and seemingly utopian. Where are the forces, where is the will to stem the tide of violence and to stop the spiral of destructive conflict?

The central committee of the WCC in its message of 1999 announcing the Decade to Overcome Violence clarified the focus of the Decade by adding the sub-title: "Churches Seeking Reconciliation and Peace", thus placing the project of the Decade in the context of the churches' calling to a "ministry of reconciliation".

> God in Christ has reconciled us to himself and entrusted us with a ministry of reconciliation. Reconciliation to God, our neighbours and ourselves, is an ongoing challenge and must be accompanied by a search for truth, justice and peace.[24]

Reconciliation has become a central term in today's public discourse. Far beyond the contexts where traditional Christian language is being used, reconciliation has become a symbol for the hopes to re-establish a viable order of peace in human community. This has not always been the case. Until not so long ago, reconciliation, if it was not understood essentially as a theological, religious concept, was understood in everyday language to refer to the settling of interpersonal disputes between marriage partners, parents and children, between friends and neighbours. It is a consequence of the fundamental crises of our century that we are now also referring to the task of resolving social and political conflicts by speaking of "reconciliation". This reflects the insight that the end of a harsh confrontation does not yet re-establish peace. Where the sources of the conflict are not being addressed, they are bound to lead to new tension and confrontation.

Reconciliation is an event between the partners of a disturbed relationship. Reconciliation has to be distinguished from the juridical conciliation of competing claims, be it in the form of a settlement out of court or in the form of compensation for damages done. Neither will reconciliation be achieved through a common – and even less through a unilateral – declaration that the old dispute should now be forgotten. It is true that both of these, i.e. the satisfaction of justified claims and the declaration to end enmity may be necessary conditions for reconciliation to come about. However, we speak of reconciliation in the full sense when both sides turn actively towards each other and engage together in reshaping their relationship. Reconciliation is not a one-time act with a beginning and an end. Rather, it has to be considered as a process which involves revisiting the divided past history with its painful memories, facing together the shame and the hurt of having the truth revealed as well as shaping a new and transformed future.

While the need for reconciliation in today's world is evident and the expectation clear that the churches should exercise a reconciling role, there is much less clarity on whether the churches are in a better position to act as agents of reconciliation than other social groups. In order to face the many questions and challenges which accompany any effort of genuine reconciliation, the churches have to begin by re-appropriating the biblical message of reconciliation in their own lives.

2. The terms in the New Testament which are rendered as "reconciliation" and "to reconcile", i.e. *katallagé* and *katallasso*, had their origin in the Greek language of the common people at that time. The Hebrew Bible has no direct equivalents. The primary context of use seems to have been the field of interpersonal relationships. It is interesting to note that the root *allasso* with the sense "to change, to transform, to exchange" leads to opposite meanings when combined with the prefix *dia* or *kata*: in the first case it can become a technical term for divorce in the sense of changing a relationship through separation; in the second case it can take the meaning of reconciliation in the sense of changing a dis-

turbed relationship through renewed communication and encounter. The usage of language thus points to the fact that reconciliation is a process that engages both partners in reciprocal interaction. Reconciliation cannot simply be declared or imposed. It involves active encounter. The Sermon on the Mount uses the term for the settling of disputes between members of the Christian community before going to the altar (Matt. 5:24). The apostle Paul speaks of "reconciliation" as the opposite of separation or divorce between marriage partners (1 Cor. 7:11). The reciprocity of giving and receiving is also expressed in the many different uses of the verb.

It is only Paul – and those parts of the New Testament bearing the marks of his theology – who adopts this "non-religious" term to interpret the saving encounter of God and humanity in Christ. He uses it in parallel with other concepts like justification, liberation, rebirth or new creation. In these other cases, he carefully establishes the link to the tradition of the Hebrew Bible, but, when using the term "reconciliation", he apparently assumes that the congregations in Rome and Corinth will understand him directly, since he is using every-day language (cf. Rom. 5:10; 2 Cor. 5:18ff.; but also Col. 1:20ff.; and Eph. 2:14ff.). The event of reconciliation for Paul is inseparably linked with the death of Jesus on the cross. The "message of reconciliation" which Paul proclaims in 2 Corinthians 5:19 is identical with the "message about the cross" (1 Cor. 1:18).

While in human relationships reconciliation is a process engaging both partners in a conflict situation, reflection on the Christian understanding of reconciliation has to start from the acknowledgment that reconciliation is offered unilaterally by God. Through Christ, the relationship between God and humanity, which had been distorted and interrupted by sin, has been restored. "All this is from God, who reconciled us to himself through Christ, and has given us the ministry of reconciliation; that is, in Christ God was reconciling the world to himself, not counting their trespasses against them, and entrusting the message of reconciliation to us"

(2 Cor. 5:18f.). We are called and invited to accept the reconciliation offered to us in Christ and to proclaim it to the world. Through Christ, a new relationship is established between those who accept this gift: strangers become citizens and aliens are recognized as members of the household of God (Eph. 2:19). Whenever divisions appear within the fellowship of the followers of Jesus Christ, in the family of his brothers and sisters, it amounts to a betrayal of the reconciliation offered by God. The healing of such divisions will not so much be the result of negotiations or mediations: relationships in the community can be healed and restored as all members together turn towards Jesus Christ. The first ecumenical conference on Life and Work in Stockholm 1925 said in its message: "The closer we come to the cross of Christ, the closer we come to one another." The World Council of Churches therefore has placed the common confession of Jesus Christ as God and Saviour at the centre of its theological basis. This is indeed the source of our reconciliation.

This understanding of the meaning of reconciliation is clearly expressed in the theme of the Second European Ecumenical Assembly at Graz in 1997: "Reconciliation – Gift of God and Source of New Life". The basic text of the Graz assembly seeks to re-appropriate the biblical message of reconciliation for our time. The text acknowledges right at the beginning that it is not to be taken for granted that the churches can claim a mandate to speak about reconciliation. Coming from an assembly of European church delegates (Catholic, Orthodox, and Protestant), the text says:

> What can "reconciliation" mean to us in Europe, when we recall that many among us still suffer from the consequences of two terrible world wars, when we grieve for hundreds of thousands of victims of armed conflicts which have wounded our continent since the fall of the Berlin wall? On what authority dare we as Christians speak of reconciliation as we approach the end of this millennium marked at its beginning by the division of the church between East and West. The answer to these questions is a renewed and common confession of faith and hope in God

> "through our Lord Jesus Christ, through whom we have now received reconciliation" (Rom. 5:11).[25]

The text then expresses joy and thanksgiving for God's offer of reconciliation in Christ, for the gift of God's mercy manifested in creation, in the person of Jesus Christ and through the power of the Holy Spirit.

> We thank God that the newness of reconciliation is at work in the world. It is the gift of the Holy Spirit, given at Pentecost, in which we experience the continuous presence of the Risen Christ in history (cf. Matt. 18:20; 28:20). We call the Spirit holy, because this Spirit not only comes from God but also has the power to make our lives holy, that is to change them fundamentally and to create new relationships. That is what *katallagé,* the Greek word for reconciliation, means (literally, a total change, a new creation, cf. 2 Cor. 2:17). Although we bear the bruises of our lack of reconciliation, we believe that this reconciling power is still at work today among us. It can already be seen in our longing for reconciliation (cf. Rom. 8:26ff.), and prepares us to let our thoughts and behaviours be transformed.

It is God's kindness that leads us to repentance and thus prepares the way for reconciliation. "Only when we are prepared to name our faults and omissions, and only when we can bring ourselves to admit our pain over injustices suffered, can we hope to free each other of these burdens and find new ways forward into the future. The reconciliation which comes from God leads us through the narrow gate of repentance into the wide valley of reconciled life." And the text addresses several of the distorted relationships ingrained in our memories as Christian communities and still burdening us today. It mentions the divisions between the churches, the long history of guilt separating Christians and Jews, the distortions in the relationships between women and men, the gulf between the generations, the conflict between rich and poor, and the abuse of creation.

Quite clearly the text states that reconciliation can never become a substitute for justice and truth.

We would like to state explicitly that the message of reconciliation does not set aside the search for justice and truth. Unfortunately, the word "reconciliation" has been cheapened for many people, because it has been used to play down and to throw a mantle of false tolerance over events that need to be opened up to public criticism. Anyone who suffers injustice must be able to count upon juridical systems upheld by uncorrupted judges and guarantee a fair legal process, so that the plaintiff's dignity may be restored and the injuries suffered may be compensated. Anyone who breaks the law must reckon with being punished. The person who has committed an injustice has no right to demand reconciliation. Neither can the readiness to forgive be expected automatically from the injured person.

Reconciliation remains an extraordinary possibility, ultimately rooted in God's act of grace.

God's reconciliation goes further than any atonement, satisfaction or correction which our legal systems can bring about, for it can heal our wounded lives and restore our self-worth. When we are touched by the power of this reconciliation, we no longer need to count and compare our sufferings, and also can stop denying and repressing guilt. As those who have received never-ending, immeasurable grace from God, we learn that grace is greater than the law.

This has consequences for relationships with other religions and cultures, for economic and political life, for the redistribution of wealth and a caring attitude to the household of life.

The text concludes with the insight that reconciliation as an act of mutual self-limitation can help us to accept the finite character of our lives and our world. We are thus called to resist

the widely accepted tendency to divide people into "winners" and "losers" and to assign values to them accordingly. We know that we are finite human beings, and yet we believe that we have the hope of a new heaven and a new earth. The horizon of expectation of the reign of God goes along with us and helps us to find our measure as mortals and to struggle against all temptations to omnipotence and superiority.

3. The message from the central committee in 1999 announcing the Decade said:

> If churches do not combine their witness for peace and reconciliation with the search for unity among themselves, they fail in their mission to the world. Leaving behind what separates us, responding ecumenically to the challenge... the churches have a unique message to bring to the conflict-ridden world... The gospel vision of peace is a source of hope for change and a new beginning. Let us not betray what has been given to us. People around the world wait with eager longing for Christians to become who we are: children of God embodying the message of love, peace with justice and reconciliation.[26]

Reconciliation is therefore first of all a challenge to the churches themselves in their present state of separation and division before they can hope to become credible agents of reconciliation in the world. There are indeed many encouraging experiences of newly discovered communion between Christians and churches which have been separated for generations and centuries. On the other hand, we also know of many instances where old divisions, prejudices and antagonisms between the churches are still alive. What is more: unreconciled memories and mutually exclusive Christian identities have been used to foment and justify militant civil conflicts as in Northern Ireland and in the Balkans. We have inherited a history of division that lives on in memories, symbols, theological affirmations and doctrinal condemnations. Particularly minority communities hold on to these memories as the basis of their identity. Fundamentalism is a phenomenon in all religions and it represents an attitude that considers the lines of separation as unchallengeable out of fidelity to inherited truth.

Therefore the warning not to be content with "cheap reconciliation" must be taken seriously. This is not to say that we should not rejoice about the restoration of ecumenical fellowship, but this new sense of communion remains fragile if it does not reach into the deeper layers of separation in the collective memory. There can be no reconciliation at the expense of truth, and there is no real reconciliation in "reconciled diversity" without a genuine change in the quality of relationships and without consequences in the attitudes of the churches towards one another. The process of reconciliation must lead to tangible change, to self-correction and to admission of mistakes and failures. Could it be the case that the difficulty in achieving lasting reconciliation between the churches is due to the fact that the guilt and errors of the past have not been uncovered and confessed? In any case, the task of reconciliation transcends the formulation of agreements and convergences. It must embrace the spiritual and ecclesial self-understanding of churches which, for centuries, have affirmed their identity over against one another.

There are several examples from recent years and decades to point to advances in ecumenical efforts at reconciliation as well as their limitations. Mention could be made of the declarations of Porvoo and Meissen regarding the establishment of communion between the Church of England and the Nordic Lutheran churches or the Protestant Churches of Germany. For twenty-five years now, the Lutheran and Reformed churches in Europe, together with the United churches and Methodist churches and the pre-Reformation churches of the Waldensians and the Czech Brethren, have lived in full fellowship with one another. More recently still, the member churches of the Lutheran World Federation and the Roman Catholic Church have solemnly accepted a joint declaration affirming that they are agreed on the basic truth of the message of justification by faith. Many more examples could be given, particularly the many cases of organic union between churches of different denominational traditions.

However, there are as many examples of situations where the task of reconciliation has barely begun. There is still tension and deep mistrust between Orthodox and Catholic Christians and churches in the former Yugoslavia and in the Ukraine, to mention only those two countries. The efforts at restoring communion between the Eastern Orthodox and the Oriental Orthodox churches have not been able to move beyond common theological affirmations.

This brief survey, therefore, does not lead to clear and unequivocal results, and there is only slight hope that the next decade might bring the decisive breakthrough. The survey shows in particular that concrete steps towards the re-establishment of communion have so far been limited largely to historic churches of the Reformation tradition, including those of the Anglican communion. The situation is rather different if we consider the relationship between the Reformation churches on the one hand and the Roman Catholic or the Orthodox churches on the other, but also regarding the relationship between these two large church families. In spite of thirty years of intensive doctrinal dialogues, there are only very few cases where an official agreement has been reached. Without the readiness for change and conversion, there will be no reconciliation. Between the church of Rome and the Orthodox churches, there is an ambiguous relationship of love and mistrust. They are closer to each other in doctrine and church order than any other church. They have recognized each other as sister churches, but the memory of a divided history of domination and forced union is still too strong and prevents a genuine reconciliation.

If ecumenical efforts at reconciliation between the churches are to move forward, we have to recognize more consciously than has been the case so far that the division between the churches and denominations are very different in character. The Protestant model of church union or of establishing full communion and church fellowship within the limits of one nation or region cannot be transferred to other church families. In the relationship with the churches of the Orthodox tradition, recent events have made us aware of the fact that we are still at the beginning of a process of overcoming alienation and misunderstanding. Among the Orthodox churches the defensive attitude that considers all other Christian churches as schismatic or heretical is still deeply rooted. We live in very different cultures and are shaped by different world-views. The process of reconciliation can only begin once we acknowledge these enduring differences. Ultimately this is true also for the relationship between the Roman Catholic and the Protestant traditions. They are close to one another as different expressions of Christianity in the West, and for this very reason they have difficulty in acknowledging their fundamental difference. Both have a tendency to consider their own way of being church as normative and to place higher demands of agreement and consensus on their partner in ecumenical dialogue than actually exists within their own communion.

Reconciliation between the churches, therefore, is a complex challenge which cannot be met through bilateral theological dialogue alone. New approaches are necessary. Ecumenical encounters between the churches have led to the insight that the churches are bound together across the lines of separation between their different traditions through their one baptism and their confession of faith. There thus already exists a real spiritual and ecclesial communion between them, even though it is not yet complete. Ecumenical dialogues between the churches are not only a means to achieve communion, but they are even now an expression of the basic communion in Christ and thus of the gift of reconciliation from God. The churches can and should recognize each other explicitly as partners and companions on the way towards full communion. This leads to the further consequence that those doctrinal controversies and condemnations of the past that have been resolved through dialogues should be considered as definitively closed and consigned to history. This would create the ecumenical space that is needed to direct attention to the challenge of common witness at the beginning of the 21st century and in this way to grow together into genuine communion.

It should have become clear that reconciliation is a process going beyond the clarification of doctrinal controversies or the overcoming of institutional barriers. Reconciliation will not come as the result of negotiations or agreements, nor can it be planned with intentional strategies. Reconciliation involves a change of heart and mind both on the personal and communal levels, a new recognition and acknowledgment of one another, and an acceptance of responsibility for one another. The new reality of a reconciled community of Christian churches will be anticipated and experienced symbolically and in prayerful celebration, before it can be defined theologically and before its institutional implications are resolved. The Decade to Overcome Violence will draw the churches closer to one another in active witness for peace and reconciliation. It should also become a space for the process of reconciliation between the churches to move forward, not so much through theological dialogue, but by promoting the change of heart and re-appropriating the spirit of reconciliation and peace.

4. This brief exposition of biblical and ecumenical insights on reconciliation and the consideration of the task of reconciliation between the churches themselves have prepared the way for us to look more closely at some of the specific challenges which the churches are facing in exercising a ministry of reconciliation. The following observations will concentrate on three of these challenges already referred to which are particularly pressing in view of recent events and experiences, i.e. reconciliation and justice, reconciliation and truth, and finally reconciliation and forgiveness.

(1) Reconciliation and justice. The profile of the ecumenical movement has been clearly marked by participation in the struggles for social justice. Again and again, churches and ecumenical assemblies have emphasized that the commitment to justice is deeply rooted in the prophetic biblical witness and has been reaffirmed forcefully by Jesus in his proclamation of God's kingdom. The "privileged option" for social justice has remained a challenge to many churches who in their self-understanding have felt a strong commitment to the priestly call to reconciliation. In 1972, M.M. Thomas, then chairman of the central committee, spoke of the tension between "the priestly ministry of liberating reconciliation and the prophetic ministry of liberating conflict". And he asked, "How can we be at once messengers of peace in a world of strife and messengers of strife in a world of false peace?"[27]

In responding to this question, the ecumenical movement has long been guided by the clear conviction that true reconciliation is only possible once justice has been achieved and those responsible for acts and structures of injustice have been brought to repentance. The strongest affirmation of this conviction that without justice there can be no true reconciliation has come through the South Africa Kairos document of 1985 with its critique of "church theology". In the perspective of the Kairos document, there can be no reconciliation in a conflict between justice and injustice, between God and the devil. This would not only be "cheap reconciliation", but would indeed constitute a "total betrayal of all that the Christian faith has ever meant". For, "trying to persuade those of us who are oppressed to accept their oppression and to be reconciled with the intolerable crimes that are committed against us is not Christian reconciliation. It is sin."[28]

After the end of the apartheid system many of those who had been involved in formulating the Kairos document became key actors in the process of the Truth and Reconciliation Commission. They were convinced that now the time had come to work for reconciliation, not by bringing the perpetrators and those responsible for the structures of injustice simply to the courts, but by obliging them to confess and disclose the full truth. Many of the victims of apartheid have been and continue to be critical of the authority given to the Truth and Reconciliation Commission to grant amnesty to those who truthfully declared their co-responsibility even without showing true repentance. They are still waiting for justice to be done to them. Others feel that their dignity has been restored by their having been able to speak publicly about the injustice they have experienced.

What we can learn from this very special case study is the insight that, just as there is a time to work for reconciliation, there may also be a time to struggle for justice. But it is not easy or obvious how to discern the times. The slow process of the international tribunals for Rwanda and Bosnia shows that the judicial systems in such extreme cases can even become a hindrance to establishing a sense of justice. They may instead deepen the divisions in the community and thus paralyze the search for urgently needed reconciliation. On the other hand, the attempts in many Latin American states or in Namibia to declare a policy of reconciliation from above by way of a generalized amnesty have created the scandalous situation of "impunity", which has become a major barrier to any genuine reconciliation in these countries.

The South African Truth and Reconciliation Commission is rooted in an African understanding of justice and reconciliation as related to the life of a given community. In African tradition, administering justice is an act of reintegrating people into the community and is therefore intimately linked with the aim of reconciliation. This corresponds to the biblical understanding of justice as the concern for right relationships. In that sense, justice and reconciliation point to two aspects or dimensions of the same process: the restoration of relationships where the rights and the dignity of all members of the community are acknowledged and protected, where the poor, the widows and orphans and even the strangers who are being deprived of their basic right to the sustenance of life are being integrated and recognized as full members of the community. Their cry for justice demands a correction of distorted relationships in order for peace and reconciliation to be restored. In this sense, peace, i.e. the situation where all are satisfied and free from basic want, is the fruit of the work of justice, as the biblical prophets proclaimed.

Obviously, it is not easy to fit this biblical (and African) thinking into our understanding of justice. Much of the ecumenical discussion has been shaped by a punitive and retributive concept of justice aimed at establishing right and wrong, attributing responsibility at the expense of promoting justice in the sense of healing and restoring the life of the community. The chairperson of the Truth and Reconciliation Commission, Archbishop Desmond Tutu, spoke of the practice of "restorative justice". We are often caught in an adversarial understanding of justice that follows the logic of power. Too often the appeal to justice and the law has been used as a political instrument to punish those perceived to be enemies instead of promoting justice as the cooperative effort to resolve a conflict or to heal the wounds and thus to prepare the way for reconciliation. To pursue justice on our own terms and at any price will not result in peace and will destroy the possibility of reconciliation. Even the application of the law alone is insufficient to bring about right relationships and lasting peace.

In the light of these observations, we may have to ask again whether we can maintain the position that the struggle for justice should legitimately have priority over the work for reconciliation. Surely there is a time for justice to be done and a time for reconciliation. These "times" do not simply follow each other in the sense that the work for reconciliation can only begin when full justice has been done. In fact, in many situations the will to bring about reconciliation is the essential condition for justice to be achieved. This was the insight guiding the Truth and Reconciliation Commission in South Africa. The experience in South Africa and the recent tragic conflicts in the former Yugoslavia and in the Great Lakes region of Africa show that this is more than an important statement of theological ethics remote from the harsh realities of the present world. More and more, we are being confronted with situations where the distinction between victims of injustice and the perpetrators becomes blurred and where the former victims become perpetrators themselves, as has happened before our eyes in Kosovo. Justice and reconciliation, therefore, cannot be separated. They are intimately linked and describe complementary needs of any human community in its search to live in right and sustainable relationships.

(2) Reconciliation and truth. Maintaining the complementary relationship between justice and reconciliation and discerning when it is time to work for justice and when to exercise the ministry of reconciliation is one of the basic challenges to the churches in their reconciling role in today's world. As the example of the Truth and Reconciliation Commission has shown, the link between reconciliation and jus-

tice points to the second challenge, i.e. uncovering the truth and struggling against distortions and lies. In fact, truth in the sense of transparency in relationships is the essential mediating link between reconciliation and justice. Uncovering the truth is an essential precondition for both reconciliation and justice because it establishes the dignity and responsibility of both victim and perpetrator. Victims cease to be mere objects of destructive power and perpetrators become persons who are being held accountable and expected to accept responsibility for their actions.

However, uncovering the truth can be dangerous. It can open up wounds and thus reinforce division. While it is true that truth can liberate, it can also become a burden that crushes both victim and victimizer. Uncovering the truth and struggling against the strategies of concealment, evasion and self-justification imply facing up to the hurt on the part of victims and guilt on the part of victimizers. Both experiences can be traumatic, and this is a challenge to the churches in their role of reconciliation. Confession and apology on the part of those responsible for acts of abuse, humiliation and destruction will not heal the trauma experienced by victims. And even on the side of the perpetrators, the demand to confess their co-responsibility may result in denial and repression, which even an offer of forgiveness by the victim cannot easily resolve.

Uncovering the truth as a precondition for reconciliation also means being prepared to face the conflict between different perspectives on the truth, the reality of deeply divided memories. Such non-reconciled memories have been the source of new conflicts in successive generations in Ireland and in the Balkans. It is true, as the wisdom of the Jewish people tells us, that remembrance is the secret of reconciliation. But when memories are divided, that is one of the major barriers to reconciliation. It then becomes the ultimate attack on human dignity to make people "disappear", thereby removing the possibility of reconciling memories.

In the more recent experience of the last decade we have also witnessed, particularly in Eastern Europe, that the effort to uncover the truth can become itself a weapon directed against political opponents. Truth in this case is deprived of its power to restore open relationships and is used as a means to claim superiority in a political struggle. Reconciling memories, on the other hand, would mean revisiting the divided past together, to share together in the collective feelings of hurt and shame, and thus to reconstruct a new present and to shape a common future. It is this active process of living in the truth, even where it is painful and costly, which Vaclav Havel, today president of the Czech Republic, in a memorable essay of October 1978 has described as the inner source of motivation of the dissident movement around Charter 77.[29] This is also the challenge that the churches will have to face in their reconciling role in today's world because the ability to live in the truth is an essential condition for reconciliation.

(3) Reconciliation and forgiveness. Obviously, there can be no reconciliation without an act of forgiveness, which is always an expression of free grace. As we have learned again in re-appropriating the biblical jubilee tradition with its appeal to cancel all debts, forgiveness can involve those in positions of power being expected to forego their rightful claims for the sake of reconciliation. Forgiveness can also mean that the victims forego their rightful claim to restitution and compensation. In all talk about forgiveness it is important to keep in mind this essential difference of perspective between those in power and the powerless, between victim and perpetrator. A generalized amnesty, as e.g. in the legislation of the "final point" in Argentina, while in formal terms claiming to represent an act of forgiveness, is in fact adding to the injury which has already been done to the victims of oppression. Forgiveness can never be imposed from a position of power, but can only be granted as a free act with the intention of restoring a broken relationship.

The profound challenge presented by the possibility of forgiveness has been described in a very penetrating way in a recent book by Geneviève Jacques with the title *Beyond Impunity: An Ecumenical Approach to Truth, Justice and Reconciliation.*[30] She writes:

Often those who have suffered violence and humiliation at the hands of other human beings or who have known the death or disappearance of their loved ones, find it virtually impossible even to think of forgiveness. How can one forgive without seeming to betray one's loved ones? How can one forgive those who refuse to admit the crimes? Who has the right to forgive? These are not mere theoretical questions. They are a source of anguished soul-searching on the part of the victims and their families – and there is no simple answer to them.

Forgiveness has often been considered to be a private moral and religious matter. The grave conflicts which have overwhelmed us at the close of the 20th century impel us also to consider forgiveness in wider and deeper social and theological terms. Recent studies on the relation between justice and forgiveness, individual and collective forgiveness, God's forgiveness and human forgiveness have explored these depths and offer guidance to those working for reconciliation.

She then identifies a number of essential dimensions to be taken into account in reflecting on reconciliation and forgiveness:

- *Forgiveness is not a legal category.* "Forgiveness does not depend on the law and administration of justice, but rather goes beyond these to take into account not only the acts committed against the victim, but also his or her continuing trauma, the lasting consequences of these violations, and the victims' relationship with those who have violated them and their loved ones."

- *Forgiveness is not to forget.* "Forgiving does not mean to ignore or erase the wrong that has been done; rather, it requires recognition both of the wrong and the wrongdoer. In the end, one may be able to forgive the criminal, but one cannot forgive the crime."

- *Forgiveness is an act of liberation.* "In forgiving, the victim decides to free himself or herself from the grief and the resentment in which she/he is imprisoned... Rather than to suppress the past, forgiveness can free victims and their descendents from the tendency of the past to dominate the present and poison the future."

- *The capacity to forgive is a gift.* "For Christians, the source of forgiveness and of the human being's capacity to forgive is found in the loving, forgiving God in whom we believe."
- *Forgiveness is part of the struggle for justice.* "Forgiveness does not forget debt, but rather *cancels* it. Thus it makes sense only when the debt is identified and is recognized by the debtor... Amnesty (from the Greek *amnesia*) legalizes forgetting. It erases, in political terms, the wrongful acts and ignores the responsibility of wrongdoers. When politicians equate the granting of amnesty with forgiving, they create an obstacle to genuine forgiveness. Government cannot act for the victims nor offer 'forgiveness' on their behalf. Amnesty does not 'cancel' a debt; it denies the existence of the debt, which is something else altogether.

5. These three challenges to the reconciling role of the churches in today's world indicate the comprehensive nature of the churches' ministry of reconciliation. It embraces the struggle for justice, the courage to uncover the truth and to resist the strategies of self-justification as well as nurturing the liberating act of forgiveness. These three essential dimensions of the process of reconciliation do not constitute a linear sequence but rather a circular process to be continued until genuine transformation of relationships is achieved, both on the moral and spiritual and on the social and political levels. As the churches engage in the Decade to Overcome Violence, they will be confronted with all of these challenges and they will discover their own tendency to compromise with the demands of justice, their own inability to live in the truth and their resistance to grant forgiveness in their relationships with each other. Only as they are prepared to be renewed in their own community life will they be able to act as agents of reconciliation in the wider community. Being engaged in a ministry of reconciliation does not mean to maintain a position of neutrality in contemporary struggles and conflicts. On the contrary: to act for reconciliation requires a profound commitment to the truth, the readiness

to claim justice for the victims and to defend the dignity and the rights of all human persons. Engaging in the ministry of reconciliation can therefore mean on occasion to take the side of and to suffer with the victims.

At the end of her book, Jacques offers a few pointers to where the commitment of the churches and of the ecumenical movement can make a difference. They can:

- humbly and perseveringly accompany the individuals, communities and leaders who are struggling to come to terms with the heritage of the past, to heal the wounds and to work to restore broken relations;
- encourage the creation of spaces for encounter where people can listen and talk to one another and experience new ways of relating to one another on the basis of truth, mutual respect and trust;
- take account of the weight and role of memory as a powerful factor of division, but also as a possible source of reconciliation if it can be freed of the passionate hatreds and myths, handed down from generation to generation, that foment division;
- promote inter-religious cooperation so that religious faiths cease to be used to legitimate or aggravate conflicts and instead offer a moral and spiritual foundation for efforts of reconciliation;
- develop the Christian message of forgiveness and the spirituality that goes with it, comprising the dimensions of truth, justice and peace, which together form the true message of reconciliation.

There is no doubt that today's world challenges the churches more than ever before to an active ministry of reconciliation. There are examples where churches, Christian communities and individual Christian people have made a difference by exercising a reconciling role, but reconciliation is not a technique which can be learned and applied as a way of peaceful resolution of conflict: it remains a gift of God and therefore the source of new life. Our prayer should be that the churches may learn again to be reconciled with God so that they can become agents of reconciliation in today's world.

III
Moral and Spiritual Formation for a Culture of Life

1. Transforming Globalization and Violence

Our globalized world is inherently conflictive. The competitive logic of the market and the confrontational logic of power politics are manifestations of a culture that considers the rule of winning and losing to be a "law of nature" from which there is no escape. The process of globalization has greatly increased this potential for conflict. It has led not only to a massive concentration but also to a diffusion of power rendering many of the traditional forms of control and legitimization ineffective. In addition, globalization has extended the range of economic, financial and media power to the whole world, thus multiplying the points of potential conflict. A violent manifestation of these conflicts is not inevitable; but any exercise of power which lacks legitimacy is in danger of provoking violent responses from those affected, especially those who have nothing more to lose.

The conflictive and therefore unstable character of the global system manifests itself also on the level of culture and identity formation. Globalization increases cultural plurality by bringing all cultures into inescapable interaction and opening up hitherto homogeneous, integrated cultural environments. While extending, via the communication media, a "virtual" culture of consumerism to all parts of the world, it offers the possibility of hybrid cultures and facilitates the emergence of "global cultural flows" (Robert Schreiter). More and more, people live in different cultures at the same time and are thus left to shape their identities with only a few points of reference. This situation has given rise to different forms of "identity politics", i.e. the determined, collective effort to mark the difference between a given community and the "others". The distinguishing marks of national, ethnic, cultural and religious identities are being used to draw boundaries and to create exclusive group loyalties in a global field of forces without direction and coherence. Globalization reinforces fundamentalist reactions, both in the political and in the religious field.

The first chapter introduced the distinction between globalization as a historical process and as a political project; the report on the Copenhagen Seminars for Social Progress argued that this distinction was necessary "to create space for human thinking and human action".[1] New thinking is indeed required if the process of globalization is to be given a constructive and humanly sustainable direction. Most of the critical analyses and reflections surveyed so far have concentrated on the impact of global capitalism and the need for new forms of global governance. Global capitalism is guided by the neo-liberal paradigm and its ideological tendency to submit all social interaction to the "laws" of "the market". This has given rise to the call for an *"alternative paradigm"* which reintroduces the historical and value dimension into social and economic analysis. The reductionist leanings of the neo-liberal ideology have produced a situation where genuine political imagination about the conditions for a "good society" seems no longer to have a place. In response, the conviction is growing that "it is time to rehabilitate ideals and utopias", pointing to the fact that even global capitalism with its promise of prosperity and happiness for the greatest number is based on a utopia that is being falsely presented as the result of natural progress. Thus, the Copenhagen seminars argue in favour of a deliberate rehabilitation of the "soft values" of solidarity, compassion and care; others, like the Ecumenical Coalition of Economic Justice, call for an alternative approach which places the economy and economic development in the wider framework of our vocation to live in right relationships with our neighbours, with the earth and with our Creator. Such an approach would be based on the affirmation of a set of basic values.[2]

We have considered the way in which globalization affects culture and religion, and in particular the thesis about the emerging "clash of civilizations". Frequently, the call for a *"new culture"* has arisen. Depending on the context, the discussion has focused on a "culture of dialogue", a "culture of solidarity", a "culture of reconciliation and peace", or a "culture of active non-violence". All of these point to a "culture of life", i.e. a culture affirming the gift of life in the midst of the social and environmental crises of our globalized world. Behind this search for a new culture stands the conviction that the present system follows certain cultural patterns which have to be transformed.

Most of the time, the term "culture" in these contexts is being used in a somewhat loose manner that requires further clarification. When reference has been made to the "culture of violence", the statements spoke of the "spirit, logic and practice of violence". Others refer to the "logic of the market" or to the "confrontational logic of war". Culture in these contexts, therefore, means a generalized pattern of thinking and acting which is rooted in certain assumptions about the dynamics of society and about human nature. This has to be distinguished from the comprehensive concept of culture used in the social sciences which refers to the overall fabric of habits, symbols, artistic representations, tools, rules of behaviour, moral values and institutions through which a given human community orders its relationship to nature, to other communities and to the world as a whole. Cultures are dynamic realities evolving and changing in the processes of learning and socialization in a community from generation to generation. In addition, cultures interact with each other. They influence and interpenetrate each other, creating new cultural forms and changing or reorienting cultural identities.

The call for a "new culture" acknowledges the fact that this process of cultural change has been intensified through globalization and that today we are confronted with a multiplicity of overlapping and competing cultures, with an implicit or explicit struggle for cultural orientation. The call for a "new culture" should, therefore, not be construed as an attempt to re-establish an integrated culture in the fundamentalist sense. Rather, it addresses the contemporary situation of comprehensive cultural change and struggle between competing "global cultural flows". It aims at cultural transformation, challenging the influence and validity of the cultural patterns being promoted through the process of globalization. The title of this book, therefore, points to the task of "transforming globalization and violence". Both are manifestations of a dominating global cultural dynamic with destructive implications. Responding to globalization and violence cannot be limited only to the establishment of new structural and institutional arrangements. It has to address the implicit cultural patterns driving the globalized system and seek to transform them by providing new cultural orientations.

Who will be the agents of this process of transformation? Again and again reference has been made to the importance of social movements and organizations in civil society as representatives and bearers of an alternative cultural dynamic. The churches and religious communities in general are being seen as vital partners in this emerging civil society at all levels. This has led Richard Falk to speak of "globalization from below" to describe different initiatives aiming at a transformation of the global system. However, he sees realistically that civil society can easily be co-opted into the dominant culture of globalization and that the different actors in civil society are often caught in the tension between either confronting or transforming the dominant culture. A confrontational stance remains at the level of critical rejection and does not transcend fundamentally the framework established by the forces of globalization. The language of prophetic criticism and rejection must, therefore, be accompanied by the language of reconstruction. What is needed is a new creative energy that can reach beyond the dominant culture and reshape or transform it. This effort, ultimately, will only be successful if it can draw on sources of cultural legitimization transcending the economic and political field. Falk, therefore, pleads for a "politically engaged spirituality", for a deliberate attempt to rediscover the religious and spiritual roots of our cultural and its values.

The project of a "global ethic", promoted by Hans Küng, is one of the most coherent attempts to spell out what a new culture would look like. Küng calls for "a culture of non-violence and respect for life; a culture of solidarity and just economic order; a culture of tolerance and a life of truthfulness; and a culture of equal rights and partnership between men and women".[3] Will this ethical and cultural reorientation drawing on humanity's religious traditions be able to transform globalization and violence? It remains largely at the level of global analysis. The attempt to formulate a "global ethic" appears to accept the conditions of the global system and to concentrate on "civilizing" or "humanizing" globalization rather than transforming it. Doubts have been expressed whether the moral and spiritual energy for transformation can be generated by formulating and proclaiming a "basic consensus on binding values, irrevocable criteria and basic attitudes which are affirmed by all religions despite dogmatic differences".[4] The new culture must be rooted in the everyday life of people and in their struggles for life. This is recognized in the emphasis on "globalization from below" and the reference to civil society.

The ecumenical movement has begun to address the challenge of globalization. Behind globalization it discerns a vision in competition with the *ecumenical vision* of the unity of humankind and of the whole inhabited earth. The ecumenical community has articulated its commitment to an oikoumene of faith and solidarity, to the life-centred vision of an "ecumenical earth". The statements and recommendations from the governing bodies of the World Council of Churches recognize, however, that calling for a new system of values alone will not be sufficient to shape a new culture, an alternative way of living, thinking and acting. Moral and ethical dilemmas arise when, in concrete situations of conflict, the demands for peace and reconciliation, for reconciliation and truth on the one hand have to be held together with the demands for justice and the defence of human rights on the other. This points to the need to strengthen the capacity of Christian communities for moral and ethical discernment. The building of a culture of reconciliation and peace has to be rooted in the concrete, local experiences of Christian communities facing situations of conflict. Generalized ethical principles will not be able effectively to transform globalization and violence. The ecumenical response to globalization should, therefore, not limit itself to a critical confrontational stance nor to articulating some generalized global vision. Rather, it should foster a "worldwide communion of particular, local embodiments of acted-out, shared, obedience to the gospel".[5]

Transforming globalization and violence requires new cultural, moral and spiritual energies. In the context of the Humanum Studies of the World Council of Churches prior to the Nairobi assembly in 1975, reference was made to the "indigenous energies" of people enabling them to resist and transform oppressive systems. The final report of the Humanum Studies explains this notion in the following terms:

> They can be discovered in and through the very experiences of human anguish whose cries we hear and whose suffering and anxiety are echoed among us. They are certainly part of and available in the human search. And they offer new ways of deepening our understanding of the gospel, just as the gospel offers ways of illuminating, judging and establishing the human significance of these resources. These are the resources of the indigenous creative energies of men and women in all their diversities and local and cultural particularities. These resources are what men and women have it in them to be and to contribute to the richness of being human because they are themselves. That is to say because they are people of a particular race, culture, history and set of experiences.[6]

Kiyoko Takeda Cho, a president of the WCC, who contributed this notion to the report, identified three roots or sources of these energies: the energy of despair, the traditional moral or religious ethos of people, and the energies of women all over the world.

Other potential sources of energy have been named, like Gandhi's concept of "truth-power" or V. Havel's determination to be "living in the truth". Further, our reflections have pointed to the biblical symbols of the sabbath and the jubilee, together with the eschatological images of hope as sources of spiritual energy for transformation. In fact, it has been argued that the challenge of globalization has to be faced at the level of symbolic power, i.e. the capacity to open up a transcendent vision of hope and meaning. These energies have to be generated and nurtured if the shaping of a new culture is to become effective. If the Christian community is to become involved in transforming globalization and violence, a deliberate attempt at moral and spiritual formation is called for. Transforming culture and personal transformation (metanoia) are inseparably linked. The apostle Paul in his letter to the Romans gives a description of this new spiritual and moral "culture" (Rom. 12:12-21), leading up to the advice: "Do not be overcome by evil, but overcome evil with good" (v.21). He opens the same chapter with the words: "Do not be conformed to this world, but be transformed by the renewing of your minds, so that you may discern what is the will of God – what is good and acceptable and perfect" (Rom. 12:2). How does such transformation of cultural attitudes and mentalities come about? Transformation calls for moral and spiritual formation.

2. Moral and Spiritual Formation

1. The issue of "moral formation" was a focal point of attention in a study process of the WCC on "Ecclesiology and Ethics" between 1993 and 1996. The insights generated in the course of this discussion, and particularly those described in the final report "Costly Obedience", are of direct relevance in this context. The study was initiated in order to link the ecclesiological and ethical reflections of the WCC Faith and Order studies on "Church and World" more closely with the ecumenical process on Justice, Peace and the Integrity of Creation. It was their aim to explore the link between what the church *is* and what the church *does*. The question emerged directly from the affirmation that the "being" of the church and not only its ethical responsibility was at stake in the justice, peace and integrity of creation process.

The study started from the affirmation that the "being" of the church was itself a "moral" reality, or, in a striking phrase, "the church not only has, but is, a social ethic, a koinonia ethic".[7] The first report ("Costly Unity", 1993) therefore spoke of the church as a "moral community". Since this terminology proved to be open to misunderstanding, the second report ("Costly Commitment", 1994) proposed to focus on the processes of moral formation and discernment.

> The categories of moral formation and discernment follow from the nature of the church and its life in the world. The churches are expected to provide important moral resources both for their own members and for the wider world. This involves, as part of the churches' overall task of spiritual formation, the moral formation of the faithful. An important part of this is training in discernment, helping church members to analyze ethical issues from the perspective of the gospel and preparing them to judge "how best to participate in the light of their faith in the moral struggles, complexities and challenges" of the present day.[8]

The churches and their members are seen as "moral agents" who participate in and influence the discourse on public policy. This is all the more important in a situation where moral discourse in society is in confusion or where public policy goes against basic moral convictions. Moral formation and discernment go together since the churches will have to be attentive to and discern the hidden agendas behind stated policy objectives and – on occasion – be prepared to advocate a life-style which challenges prevailing cultural values.

The third report ("Costly Obedience", 1996) takes this exploration further by placing the moral formation taking place in and through the Christian community in the context of pluralistic societies with competing and overlapping moral and cultural orientations, a situation which makes it difficult to arrive at common values. How can Christians in such a setting "make a difference" or even become agents of transformation? This question prompts a further clarification of the meaning of "formation":

> Moral formation is a nurturing process in which a certain sense of identity, a certain recognition of community, and a certain pattern of motivation, evolve... Such formation can be the gradual work of culture and upbringing, or it may be self-conscious and intentional. Any community of which we are members "forms" us in the sense of orienting us to the world in a certain way, encouraging certain kinds of behaviour and discouraging others. A focus on formation points us towards... the complex "thickness" of lives actually lived. The "formation" discussion inevitably turns sooner or later to the subject of "spirituality"... With modernity's characteristic "affirmation of everyday life", "spirituality" has also come to mean the depth dimension of daily existence cultivated by both meditative and moral practices. The meditative and the moral, indeed, cannot be separated. They are part of one whole cloth. Spirituality can now mean the whole shape, the shared fabric, of our lives in God.[9]

Moral and spiritual formation shape a certain way of living and of seeing life. However, in a situation where several moral and cultural environments overlap and where globalization colonizes human life, Christians need particular guidance for moral discernment. This is important especially in situations threatened by violence and warfare, where Christians and churches often feel powerless to resist the appeal for solidarity with their national or ethnic community. Instead of being agents of transformation, the churches simply conform to the dominant patterns of their cultural or national contexts. The report points to the South African Truth and Reconciliation Commission as a rare example of a deliberate process of formation towards truth and reconciliation in church and society.

In its second report the study had described the result of moral formation as shaping the *"ethos* of the household of faith", i.e. "the way of life, the distinctive patterns of thinking, feeling and acting, which characterize those who live within that 'household'".[10] The word "household" is an attempt to translate the Greek term *oikos,* which is also the root of the concept of the "oikoumene*"*. The "household of faith" points in the first instance to the local community, but also beyond it to the worldwide church, and it relates the life and witness of the church to the economic and social realities of the world. With the concept of the household of faith the study tries to indicate the linkage between local and global perspectives. Moral and spiritual formation has to take shape in the local community, but it also has to generate the capacity to discern the connectedness between diverse local settings and the specific moral challenges arising in the global context.

The first report of the study already included these observations:

> The "local" means different things in different circumstances. It may mean a neighbourhood, or a nation, or a region of the world. And sometimes an issue may be global in its importance, yet not susceptible of any single explanation or formula so varied are its ramifications in different places. Sometimes a global issue is such that it comes to expression most clearly in some particular locality, whose Christian people then have special responsibility for defining its significance for the rest of the oikoumene. Sometimes an essentially local issue can only be clearly seen when its global aspects are grasped. We need new forms of expression for both the local and the global, depending on the issue and the setting in which it can most trenchantly be formulated. In this connection it is important to recall the theme of catholicity as an attribute of the church...[11]

Generating understanding and sensitivity for this inter-relationship between the local and the global is an essential part of moral formation in an age of globalization.

Moral formation will have to give particular attention to shaping a new understanding of human responsibility, both individually and collectively. From different sides the plea has been made to supplement the Universal Declaration of Human Rights with a Declaration of Human Responsibilities. In fact, in a cultural setting favourable to the individual's pursuit of self-interest, the demand for the recognition of one's "rights" irrespective of the rights and needs of others can lead to social disintegration. The legitimacy of human rights entails, at least, the responsibility to consider the consequences of their implementation for others in the community or for other communities. The situation of global interdependence sharpens the need for a new appreciation of human responsibility. Actions and decisions in one place potentially have repercussions worldwide. Modern forms of production, mobility and consumption have destructive consequences for natural life-cycles. This has been demonstrated dramatically in the international debate on climate change. We have to become conscious of our responsibility to protect and safeguard the viability of life of other human beings and human communities and the natural life-cycles on which human survival depends. Moral formation will have to be oriented towards creating "sustainable communities".

This "new culture" could therefore also be described as a "culture of responsibility", and the values being promoted can be understood as criteria for the exercise of that responsibility. But the moral challenge and the need for discernment are intensified in the context of globalization. It becomes less and less possible to evaluate and anticipate the consequences and repercussions of particular actions or decisions on other communities, on future generations or natural life systems. Equally legitimate and central values can get into conflict with each other. A case in point is the tension between the commitment to peace and peaceful resolution of conflict and the obligation to protect the rights and lives of people in situations of armed violence. Precaution, prudence and discernment are needed to search for ways of action that do not sacrifice either of the values but recognize their inter-dependence.

2. Moral formation and spirituality are closely interrelated. This affirmation of the study process on ecclesiology and ethics needs to be developed further. In fact, the process of cultural transformation draws on spiritual energies, even where this is not acknowledged. The report on "Costly Obe-dience" spoke of spirituality as the "depth dimension of daily existence cultivated by both meditative and moral practices".

In the period between the assemblies at Vancouver (1983) and Canberra (1991) the search for "a spirituality for our times" was the focus of intensive ecumenical dialogue and reflection.[12] The report of section IV of the Canberra assem-bly under the title: "Holy Spirit – Transform and Sanctify Us!" summarizes the affirmations on ecumenical spirituality arising from these dialogues in the following terms:

> Spirituality – in its manifold forms – is about receiving energy
> for life, being cleansed, inspired and set free, in every way
> being conformed to Christ. An ecumenical spirituality for our
> times should be incarnational, here and now, life-giving, rooted
> in the scriptures and nourished by prayer; it should be commu-
> nitarian and celebrating, centred around the eucharist,
> expressed in service and witness, trusting and confident. It will
> inevitably lead to suffering; it is open to the wider oikoumene,
> joyful and hopeful. Its source and guide is the action of the Holy
> Spirit. It is lived and sought in community and for others. It is
> an ongoing process of formation and discipleship.[13]

The aspects of this description which are of particular signifi-cance for our reflection are the understanding of spirituality as energy for life; its incarnational character or rootedness in the here and now, in the world of human life; its orientation towards community and its openness to the wider oik-oumene.

Gwen Cashmore and Joan Puls, animators of this ecu-menical dialogue after the Nairobi assembly, build their introduction to an ecumenical spirituality around the notions of openness, connectedness and earthedness.[14] *Openness* is the ability to transcend one's self, one's horizon; it is the willingness to make room for the other, to open oneself to the action of the Spirit; it is the manifestation of humility, the readiness not to insist on being right but to make oneself vulnerable and to be transformed in the encounter with others. *Connectedness* is the recognition that all life is sustained by bonds of community. All life participates in a delicate web of interconnections, in the flow of energy originating in God the Creator. The networks of communication and interaction facilitated by globalization by which it is spreading are only a rediscovery and reflection of the most basic connectedness at the root of all life. Connectedness as a mark of spirituality finds its expression in the recognition and practice of cooperation, reciprocity and mutuality over against a culture based on self-interest and competitiveness. Connectedness shapes the ethos of non-violence: it affirms the opponent or enemy as a potential partner in a relationship of mutuality and communication. It also marks the quality of relationships, as mentioned before with reference to catholicity, and points to that spiritual energy which transforms relationships. *Earthedness*, finally, binds the ecumenical spirituality to the everyday conditions of life at a given time and place, recognizing its finiteness and limitations, in constant dialogue with its cultural and social environment. An earthed spirituality takes seriously the temptation to worship false gods; it accepts the task of "discerning the spirits" and nurtures the capacity for resistance, for endurance and staying power in the struggle to unmask the powers and principalities of this world (cf. Eph. 6:10-13).

From an Asian perspective, Masao Takenaka has pointed to the way in which images and symbols rooted in a local culture can nurture the power of spiritual imagination and shape the human sense of responsibility. In an essay on Asian spirituality, entitled *God Is Rice*, he interprets a poem by the Korean Christian poet Kim Chi Ha, "Heaven Is Rice", which meditates on the highly symbolic character of rice as the daily food for people in Asia. "The Chinese character for peace *(wa)* literally means harmony. It derives from two words: one is rice and the other is mouth. It means that unless we share rice together with all people, we will not have peace. When every mouth in the whole inhabited world is filled with daily food, then we can have peace."[15] This leads him to two important considerations:

> When we say that God is rice we do not mean we should worship rice. We take rice as the symbol of God's gift of life... Second, if we acknowledge that God is rice, the symbolic source of the whole creation, and if we accept nature as our companion, rather than an object to be conquered or exploited, there will be a decisive change in our attitude towards the ecological issues.[16]

This approach to spirituality as rooted in the culture of people, especially the people of the "third world", is reflected also in the report of the 1992 assembly of the Ecumenical Association of Third World Theologians in Nairobi.[17] In his introduction, K.C. Abraham, referring to the same poem by Kim Chi Ha, says:

> The cry of the third world is a cry for life. It is a cry for freedom and dignity that constitute life as human. It is cry for the rice and bread that sustain life, as well as for the community that symbolizes and grows from rice and bread eaten in company... Rice and bread for one person alone may not be spiritual because it may be selfish... Or, in the words of Nicholas Berdyaev, rice for myself alone may be unspiritual, but rice for my hungry sister and brother is spiritual. Thus, our cry for life is a cry for the bread and the rice of life and for the spirituality of all the activities, processes, and relationships bound up with producing and sharing rice and bread. Ours is a cry for a spirituality of and for life.

The statement of the assembly, entitled "A Cry for Life", refers especially to the cries of women, of black, indigenous and Hispanic peoples as well as to the ecological movement. It states:

> We live our spirituality in creative response to the cry for life, the cry for God. We celebrate our spirituality in songs, rituals

and symbols which show the energizing Spirit animating the community to move together in response to God... There is no room for romanticizing spirituality. It is a cry for life, a power to resist death and the agents of death. Spirituality is the name we give to that which provides us with the strength to go on, for it is the assurance that God is in the struggle.

And then the statement describes this spirituality as a spirituality of commitment rooted in a radical conversion to the God of liberation and life and able to inspire the search for alternatives beyond capitalism and socialism.

We need to keep this wider understanding of a "spirituality of and for life" in mind as we return to the study on ecclesiology and ethics which, in its final report, has contributed a fresh interpretation of the ecumenical movement as a network of spiritual interconnectedness. It proposes an understanding of the oikoumene as an "energy-field" of mutual resonance and recognition generated by the Holy Spirit. It can be seen as

a conscious *mutual* recognition of the resonating patterns and configurations of activity that follow from the Spirit's working. Before there can be an articulable oikoumene there is the resonance in which diverse local communities of faith recognize and share the forming, energizing power of the Spirit. By choosing resonance and recognition as our metaphors we are able to turn to a biblical formula found in the Johannine literature... The sheep know the shepherd's voice (John 10:3; cf. Rev. 3:20)... Discipleship means hearing, being drawn, being formed, by the voice: not just its sound but also the content, the authentic note of a way of speaking by which we are shaped, attesting to an identifiable way of being in the world, yet a way of being having many different forms... The focus of ecumenical recognition is that the other community has an acted commitment analogous to one's own, and one's own commitment is analogous to the other. The analogy exists because of the shared recognition-pattern of moral practice in the Spirit. People... recognize that others "have the same spirit"... Such recognition is something holistic... It is recognition of a lived reality: a sense of moral communion. This is what oikoumene means.[18]

The oikoumene, thus, becomes a space where continuous moral and spiritual formation takes place in the process of sharing commitments, challenges and experiences. In particular, the ecumenical community promotes critical discernment of the spirits and of ethical choices in the global context since it makes the members of the community aware of the consequences of moral and ethical choices in one place for other members of the community. It sharpens the sense of responsibility and the practice of mutual accountability.

3. There are several instances in the recent history of the World Council of Churches where the validity of this interpretation of the oikoumene has been tested and confirmed. This includes the Ecumenical Decade of the Churches in Solidarity with Women and the campaign "Peace to the City". Both were processes based on dynamic interaction and exchange between local communities, questioning, challenging and encouraging each other rather than following a centrally organized programme.

There is one further example, the "Theology of Life" programme of the former WCC Unit on Justice, Peace and Creation, where the implications of this interpretation for the search for a new culture of life have been extensively considered. The programme took as its starting point the tension that had emerged during the world convocation at Seoul (1990) between a global analysis of the threats to life and the specificity of local struggles for life and survival. The ten affirmations and the commitments accepted by the Seoul convocation go beyond a position of prophetic criticism and the call to resistance: they should be seen as initiating the action of reconstruction, of envisaging a new culture of solidarity and sharing, a culture of active non-violence and respect for the integrity of all life. They go beyond the values shaping the dominant culture and provide the framework for a process of transformation. It was the objective of the "Theology of Life" programme to expose these affirmations to a reality- and validity-test in different local contexts and to identify instances where this new culture of life is already being shaped. Challenging the affirmation of the advocates of the neo-liberal paradigm that "there is no alternative", the 23 case studies, each taking one of the ten affirmations from Seoul as an interpretative framework, produced impressive evidence of the lived alternatives which motivate people in their struggles.

The programme was based on the methodological assumption that exposing the different local struggles to each other and linking them would deepen people's understanding in each of the locations at the same time. Rather than asking for analytical case studies presenting the situation in a given place, the programme encouraged a narrative, community-based approach capturing the stories, symbols and practices in which people express their hopes and making visible the resources of tradition and collective identity from which they draw energies in their struggles for life.

It was the aim of the programme to discover new ways of linking the local and the global and thus to develop the language and form of communication which will be needed for a process of cultural transformation. This is well expressed in an assessment by the case study coordinators:

> We need theological and ethical tools to deal with fragmentation, to tap into the creativity and resources of the people of God and their traditions, to understand sources of spiritual growth and social survival. Such a comprehensive theological and ethical revival will give new impetus to the capacity of the WCC to witness to its ecumenical vision. TOL [theology of life]... can be envisioned as an open space, a theatre for the presentation of the gifts and contributions of others. It is a safe arena, though not without risk. It is a space of acceptance, of understanding, of affirmation. Such a context or space is a necessary precondition to dialogue. Dialogue marks out the conciliar space. Such a framework opens up exciting possibilities for ecumenical dialogue and ecumenical social thought and action.[19]

The vision of an open, ecumenical space found its tangible expression in the *Sokoni* event in January 1997 which brought all the participants in the programme together in a traditional African market setting, offering opportunities to listen to the stories of others, to discover similarities and differences and to grow together across boundaries, sharing life with life.

In an inspiring address to the central committee of the WCC in September 1997 under the title "Glimpses of the New Ecumenical Movement", Margot Kässmann described the important lessons learnt from this process and from the Decade of Churches in Solidarity with Women.[20] She emphasized first of all: "We have gained a new approach to the relation of local and global." In particular, the *Sokoni* event provided the setting where the global agenda was being discussed among local people; the local experience became the mirror of the worldwide issues. The differences between the local responses became the "medium to see one's reality in a new way". In order for this to happen,

> we have to learn how to listen. Learning how to listen includes creating a safe, protected space for others to talk. What is different can stay different. We do not have to force it into our own paradigm in order to give it validity... Diversity in itself is not the goal. Nobody leaves the encounter of the other unchanged.

Then she added, "We have caught a glimpse of what the church might be: a community of lovers of life!" The *Sokoni,* creating an open circle in which all were able to participate and to speak, nurtured the vision of the church

> as an open space, where life has space. The church as a safe space where women are encouraged to speak instead of being silenced... Life, God's greatest, most wonderful gift at the centre of the encounter of God's people. In fact solidarity, community, is growing out of the threat to life that occurs in different forms all over the world. The Decade and the *Sokoni* have shown that the church can be the centre of this growing community. Even more, the church comes into being... Today I think we should challenge the globalization of economy and politics with the solidarity of Christians around the world, people of faith around the world. The church of Christ overcomes all boundaries of class, gender, nation, ethnic group. It is a true community valuing life.

Finally, she ended with the call: "Let us dare to give shape to the vision of an ecumenical earth." Offering this vision as the "legacy" of the whole process she indicated three elements for further exploration:

- Life is the key element of that vision... Life in all its fullness is probably the deepest longing of human beings. Life is bread and shelter, education and health. And it is more than bread alone, it means respect and dignity, justice and peace, love and truth. Life in fullness means inclusion, participation, belonging. And life is a much wider concept than the human community alone.
- Secondly, the theological exploration of "oikos" might lead us further along the way... Oikos is a key element of talking about local reality as well as about earth community as an all-inclusive life form.
- Thirdly, the exploration of the meaning of household will also be a key element. The global does not substitute for the local – they live in each other. This vision is a vital contribution to life on this planet. It is a challenge to a globalization that simply pushes aside the local reality of people.

3. The Vision of the Oikoumene

These reflections on cultural transformation, about the building of a new culture and the processes of moral and spiritual formation which take place in each local community and in the ecumenical community worldwide lead us finally once again to the vision of the oikoumene. Ecumenical statements have frequently affirmed that the ecumenical vision stands critically over against the vision implicit in the project of globalization. The ecumenical vision has been expressed as commitment to "the unity of humankind and the whole inhabited earth"; as a "life-centred vision of an ecumenical earth"; and as a "vision of the fullness of life for all". The oikoumene has been interpreted as a community of "faith and solidarity" or as representing "a sense of moral communion". All these phrases point in a similar direction but they remain at the level of fairly abstract concepts and would need to be unpacked in order to generate a process of moral formation and cultural transformation. Apart from the resources that have already been used in developing the argument so far, a number of authors have made contributions to this discussion which could help in developing the vision of the oikoumene.[21]

1. Most of the attempts to interpret and bring alive the ecumenical vision go back to the original meaning of oikoumene, which is "the whole inhabited earth". This leads to a new understanding of the earth as *oikos*, i.e. as habitat or habitation for all life. The earth is the common space for all living things, the "household of life".

> Habitat is the core meaning of all *eco* words: economy, ecology, ecumenicity itself. *Oikos* – earth as a vast but single household of life – means the capacity for survival, that is, sustainable habitat. It means space and the means for the living of all living things. Without adequate hospitable habitat, nothing lives. Not only humans, but all life forms need carefully fitted habitats.[22]

The conflict between the ecumenical vision and the vision behind economic globalization is unavoidable: both have the same root *oikos* and have to respond to the criterion to maintain the earth "inhabitable". Economics in its most basic meaning is the knowledge of the material requirements of the household of life and how they are to be met. "The basic task of any economy, then, is *the continuation of life*, though no economist has put it this way for ages."[23] The economist *(oikonomos)* is the trustee and manager of the household of life who knows about the fragility and limits of the earth as habitation for life. Ecology, on the other hand, is the knowledge of the inter-related dynamics of the household, of its sustainability and of the "logic of life", which can enter into conflict with the logic of power or the logic of the market.

Finally, and important for our reflection about moral formation, the biblical writers speak of *oikodomé*, the constant effort to maintain and build up the *oikos* of life, to restore those parts which have been damaged.[24] Larry Rasmussen states:

> For the biblical writers *oikodomé* never loses its focus on the particular community at hand and its well-being. The global does not substitute for the local. Just as the understanding of "ecumenical" in the early church designated the *whole* church in *each* place, so *oikodomé* refers to the global in the local community. The local is the basic unit of the global. Microcosm and macrocosm live within each other. They share the same dwelling. *Oikodomé*, moreover, is understood by the first Christians as forging and sustaining a specific *moral* culture precisely at a turning point in history, at a time when a "new age" was taking shape, one that required moral and religious communities attuned to it.[25]

He points out that the early Christian community also included in its instruction of new members the rules for the upbuilding and the management of the household. While the primary focus of this process of moral formation was the concrete, local community, it was also intended to raise their awareness of the unity of the household of life, the whole oikoumene of God.

Several attempts have been made to translate and apply these insights about the roots of the ecumenical vision in order to establish criteria for ecumenical efforts to transform our globalized world. Geiko Müller-Fahrenholz reinterprets the ecumenical process for Justice, Peace and the Integrity of Creation as an invitation "to enter into an ecodomical covenant". He sees truth, solidarity and endurance as the focal points of the moral and spiritual task lying ahead of the ecumenical community.[26] Rasmussen summarizes the moral norms arising from this discussion "as norms of and for sustainability". These norms include criteria already mentioned, such as participation, sufficiency, equity, accountability, material simplicity and spiritual richness, responsibility and subsidiarity.[27]

This interpretation of sustainability which focuses on the conditions for sustainable living in community and within the context of the natural world takes issue with the notion of "sustainable development" which has become the officially proclaimed response to the social, economic and ecological crises created by the process of globalization. "Sustainable development" remains bound to the logic of growth and progress inherent in the economic system. "Sustainable community" describes a change of direction sensitive to the logic of the household, the logic of life. The Canberra assembly addressed this tension in very clear terms. The report of section I under the theme "Giver of Life – Sustain Your Creation" includes a section on "rethinking economics" which says:

> What we need... is first of all a new concept of value, based not on money and exchange but rather on *sustainability* and *use*. Humankind has failed to distinguish between growth and development. While advocating "sustainable development" many people and groups in fact often have found themselves promoting "growth". Growth for growth's sake – the continued addition to what already is present – is the strategy of the cancer cell. Growth for growth's sake is increase in size without control, without limit, in disregard for the system that sustains it. It ultimately results in degradation and death.[28]

2. Sustainability and sustainable community as the criteria of the moral culture inherent in the ecumenical vision take us

back once again to the ecumenical community itself as the space where this process of formation and transformation is to take shape. The report "Costly Obedience" from the study on ecclesiology and ethics interpreted the oikoumene as a space for mutual recognition and sharing, creating a "sense of moral communion". The "Theology of Life" programme provided examples of this mutual recognition and sharing. This sharing took place not so much through a common conceptual framework but rather by stories and symbols. Rasmussen, Takenaka and others place central importance on symbols, images and metaphors which convey insights about what is essential for a viable, sustainable way of life. People communicate through symbols, images and stories rather than through concepts. Symbols express hope and thus become a source of power. This is particularly true for our symbols and images of God, of creation and redemption. "Symbols can communicate a mystique, a mystique that discloses how the ultimate mysteries of existence are manifest in the universe."[29]

The report "Costly Obedience" prefers to speak of "signposts" or "markings" which can guide the process of moral formation.

> Certain signposts emerge in the process of living out identifying factors of moral formation... Terms like "justice" and "peace" function in the ecumenical movement to help persons with analogous experiences find one another, and thus support, enable, encourage, and empower one another.[30]

The traditional marks of the church function in the same way: they mark the space for communion to grow.

> Communion means a recognition that we are living the same stories in forms, both liturgical and moral, which manifest the mystery, the transcending ground, of what is historically manifest.

In the same manner the biblical symbols of the sabbath and the jubilee have served as signposts or markings generating "a sense of communion". They provide pointers for mutual identification and recognition, a language which releases spiritual energy for the task of transformation.

The report "Costly Obedience" then continues to apply this understanding of moral communion to the WCC itself. Though not itself that moral communion,

> it *is* a community of churches praying to receive the spiritual gifts which such communion in moral witnessing will require... The WCC needs to mark, maintain, indeed *be* a space where the ecclesio-moral communion... can come to expression, where language is constantly sought to express the reality more fully, where common actions are conceived which embody the needed moral witness, and where an ecumenical formation takes place which gives growing density, increasing fullness, to it.

The report interprets the ten affirmations from the Seoul convocation as means to "create moral space for the 'mutual up-building' or *oikodomé* towards a common witness that now becomes a primary calling for the Christian churches of the world". And then the report concludes with the following appeal:

> The World Council of Churches, if possible in concert with other ecumenical bodies, should continue to promote the mutual up-building of such a visible moral communion, towards a vision of the church as moral "household of life"... A network of moral communication among the churches could begin to function as a kind of "third force" to counter the hegemony of purely economic and political energies. The initiative to create such a "third force" could include critical, provisional, alliances with others who seek compatible goals.

Such alliances are beginning to be formed in the context of the World Social Forum.

3. "Ecumenical earth" or "the household of life" describes spaces for life. The *oikos* character of the oikoumene has led to a more intentional reflection about ways to create and open up an "ecumenical space" and to reclaim the room needed for true encounter, for trust and understanding to

grow, for deliberation and discernment to develop, for a sense of moral communion to emerge. Reclaiming space and time for true life in sustainable community is one of the critical dimensions in the effort to transform globalization.

Globalization has a profound impact on the human experience of space and time. It both expands and compresses space and time. Boundaries become obsolete and distances shrink. People, goods, knowledge and information move in all directions. Globalization invades protected spaces of human life and weakens or removes the traditional landmarks of identity and distinctiveness. Through the electronic communication networks the experience of space as extension is radically compressed; a sense of proximity and apparent neighbourhood is being created in the virtual space of the cyber-world.

In the same way globalization affects our sense of time. The immediacy of electronic communication creates an impression of simultaneity. Time is reduced to a present with only a short-term view of the future. Under the pressure of high-speed living people can no longer afford to "waste time", to wait for the right moment, to take time for reflection, deliberation and discernment, or simply take time for living. Time has to be planned and managed. While the future becomes a realm of undetermined possibilities, the past becomes obsolete. Communities lose their memory, their sense of tradition and their wisdom. Where change becomes the only constant factor, people's awareness of history, of the continuum of life as past, present and future, disappears.

Any process of moral and spiritual formation needs space and time, a safe space

> where people can learn how to receive one another's stories, and be open to learning from others again and again how to recontextualize their way of receiving wisdom, insights and criticisms from across the boundaries of difference.[31]

Telling one's story, sharing cries of anguish or energies of hope can make people vulnerable. They must be given space to be themselves and time to wait for the right moment. Sustainable communities need space and time for genuine encounter and dialogue. Transformation does not come without pain and labour. The pressure to reach immediate decisions narrows the space and reduces the time for genuine listening and learning. In particular, peaceful resolution of conflict or efforts at reconciliation require time and space. The global media create the expectation of an instant response, which reduces the possibility of reconciliation.

The ecumenical community represents a worldwide network of local communities rooted in their respective social, cultural and historic contexts. In responding to globalization it can build on decades of experience in living with differences and disagreements, in challenging and empowering each other, and in practising solidarity. It has been engaged in the effort to open space for those who are pushed to the margin or excluded. This will become one of its most important contributions in a time of globalization. "Ecumenical space" could become a leading symbol for initiatives to offer space and time for people seeking to discern the "signs of the time" and searching for moral orientation and spiritual guidance. In the words of Lewis Mudge, the churches "can provide not only material hospitality to the stranger, but also spiritual hospitality: a sanctuary of meaning for those who, for many reasons – intellectual, religious, political – are unable to confess the source of this meaning".[32] Sometimes the churches in the ecumenical fellowship have indeed offered to the wider secular community the space for reflecting more deeply on the moral and spiritual dimensions of justice and injustice, reconciliation, human rights and peace-building. As Mudge says:

> Churches can and should offer a sort of metaphorical space in the world for those, believers or otherwise, who believe that human society can overcome its violent origins, its continuing resentment and mistrust, and come to realize its true calling to become the beloved community envisioned in the biblical story. The churches exist to *hold open* a social space in which society's existing structures and practices can be seen for what they

are and in which human community can be articulated in a new way, a space in which the metaphors of common life can be exposed to their transcendental ground.[33]

This is, indeed, a vision that could inspire the process of transforming globalization and violence.

Notes

I. TRANSFORMING GLOBALIZATION

[1] *The New Catholicity*, Maryknoll NY, Orbis, 1997, p.11.

[2] *Building a World Community: Globalization and the Common Good*, Jacques Baudot ed., Copenhagen, 2000, p.44.

[3] *Ibid.*, p.45.

[4] *The Economic Consequences of the Peace*, London, 1919, pp.6f. (credit is given for this quote to Elizabeth Ferris).

[5] Eric Hobsbawm, *Age of Extremes: The Short Twentieth Century 1914-1991*, London, M. Joseph, 1994, p.87.

[6] See in particular *Christian Faith and the World Economy Today: A Study Document from the World Council of Churches*, WCC, 1992; Richard Dickinson, *Economic Globalization: Deepening Challenge for Christians*, WCC, 1998; Rob van Drimmelen, *Faith in a Global Economy: A Primer for Christians*, WCC, 1998.

[7] *Building a World Community*, pp.55f.

[8] "Political Economy, Ethics and Theology: Some Contemporary Challenges", report of a consultation in Zürich, Switzerland, 5-10 June 1978, in *Ecumenism and a New World Order*, Marcos Arruda ed., WCC, 1980, pp.7ff.

[9] James D. Wolfensohn, "Building an Equitable World", address to the board of governors, Prague, 26 Sept. 2000, p.9.

[10] See *Human Development Report 1992*, New York/Oxford, 1992, pp.74ff.

[11] Inge Kaul, Isabelle Grunberg, Marc Stern eds, *Global Public Goods: International Cooperation in the 21st Century*, Oxford, Oxford UP, 1999.

[12] *Ibid.*, p.453.

[13] *Justice: The Heart of the Matter. An Ecumenical Approach to Financing for Development*, Toronto/Geneva, Jan. 2001, pp.1f.

[14] Richard Falk, *Religion and Humane Global Governance*, New York, Palgrave, 2001, p.72.

[15] This is the programmatic formulation used by Falk, *op. cit.*, pp.4ff., 13ff., 74f., 135ff.

[16] See *Building a World Community*. This and the following references on pp.34, 35 and 37 are to pp.49, 86, 102, 99, 18, 31, 16, 121, 123.

[17] See Richard Falk and Andrew Strauss, "On the Creation of a Global People's Assembly: Legitimacy and the Power of Popular Sovereignty", *Stanford Journal of International Law*, 36, 2, 2000, pp.1ff.

[18] Richard Falk, "Realizing the Copenhagen Vision: The Political Imperative", in *Building a World Community*, p.164.

[19] *Religion and Humane Global Governance*, p.75.

[20] Schreiter, *The New Catholicity*, p.16.

[21] *Religion and Humane Global Governance*, ch. 5, pp.101-22.

[22] This thesis was first developed in an article and subsequently elaborated in a book. See Samuel Huntington, *The Clash of Civilizations and the Remaking of World Order*, New York, Simon & Schuster, 1996.

[23] For further discussion of the Huntington thesis cf. part II, ch. 3, pp.99.

[24] "Striving Together in Dialogue: A Muslim-Christian Call to Reflection and Action", discussion paper, WCC Inter-Religious Relations and Dialogue, 2001, para. 16, p.6.

[25] See "A Global Ethic and Global Responsibilities: Two Declarations", Hans Küng and Helmut Schmidt eds, London, 1998.

[26] Hans Küng, *A Global Ethic for Global Politics and Economics*, New York, Oxford UP, 1998, pp.92f.; for a more developed reflection on Küng's proposal cf. my paper "Global Order and Global Ethic", *Concilium*, 4, 2001, pp.19ff., and also the other contributions to this issue.

[27] Küng, *A Global Ethic*, p.111.

[28] See *Our Global Neighbourhood*, New York, Oxford UP, 1995; cf. also *Crossing the Divide: Dialogue among Civilizations*, New York, UN, 2001.

[29] Bert Hoedemaker, "The Unity of Humankind: Problems and Promises of an Indispensable Ecumenical Theme", *The Ecumenical Review*, 50, 3, 1998, p.307.

[30] See the Dogmatic Constitution on the Church of the Second Vatican Council, *Lumen Gentium*, para. 1; see also *The Uppsala Report*, Norman Goodall ed., WCC, 1968, section I, "The Holy Spirit and the Catholicity of the Church", para. 20.

[31] Hoedemaker, "The Unity of Humankind", p.310.

[32] See van Drimmelen, *Faith in a Global Economy*; Dickinson, *Economic Globalisation*.

[33] *Faith in a Global Economy*, p.135.

[34] This and the following references on pp.58, 59 and 60 are to *Together on the Way*, Diane Kessler ed., WCC, 1999, pp.177ff., 183,258f., 260,261,146f.

[35] *Central Committee Minutes*, 1999, p.93.

[36] *Central Committee Minutes*, 2001, p.123.

[37] *Ibid.*, p.124; cf. also the recent brochure *Economic Globalization: A Critical View and an Alternative Vision*, WCC/JPC, 2002, which develops further the programme implications of the recommendation by the central committee.

[38] Schreiter, *The New Catholicity*, pp.118f.

[39] *The Uppsala Report*, section I, para. 7.

[40] *Ibid.*, para. 18.

[41] The following paragraphs are adapted from my paper published under the title "Catholicity Revisited", in *Agape: Etudes en honneur de Mgr. Pierre Duprey*, Annalecta Chambesiana, 3, Chambesy/Genève, 2000, pp.111-36.

[42] Schreiter, *The New Catholicity*, p.128.

[43] *Now Is the Time. The Final Document and Other Texts of the World Convocation on "Justice, Peace and the Integrity of Creation"*, Seoul, 1990, WCC, 1990, p.12.

II. TOWARDS A CULTURE OF RECONCILIATION AND PEACE

[1] See *Gathered for Life*, David Gill ed., WCC, 1983, pp.130ff.

[2] See *Now Is the Time: Final Document and Other Texts of the World Convocation on "Justice, Peace, and the Integrity of Creation"*, *Seoul, 1990*, WCC, 1990, pp.17,29.

[3] The following observations draw largely on my paper "Peace on Earth: New Visions and New Praxis", consultation on non-violent approaches to conflict resolution, Corrymeela, Northern Ireland, June 1994, in *Overcoming Violence: WCC Statements and Actions 1994-2000*, S. Eskidjian and S. Estabrook eds, WCC, 2000, pp.102ff.

[4] The following paragraphs are taken largely from my report as general secretary to the WCC central committee meeting in Geneva, 1999, in *Overcoming Violence*, pp.123ff.

[5] *Central Committee Minutes*, 1995, p.50.

[6] *Central Committee Minutes*, 1996, p.176.

[7] *Central Committee Minutes*, 1995, pp.265ff., esp. pp.272f.

[8] *Gathered for Life*, p.132.

[9] *Together on the Way*, Diane Kessler ed., WCC, 1999, p.145.

[10] *Central Committee Minutes*, 1999, p.92.

[11] Based on a lecture published in German in *Dekade zur Überwindung von Gewalt 2001-2010. Impulse*, Fernando Enns ed., Frankfurt, Lembeck, 2001, pp.11 ff.; cf. also Margot Kässmann, *Overcoming Violence: The Challenge to the Churches in All Places*, WCC, 2000.

[12] This and the following references on pp.84, 85 and 86 are to *Overcoming Violence: WCC Statements*, pp.50, 51, 51f, 52, 54f., 54.

[13] Baltimore, Johns Hopkins UP, 1979.

[14] This and the following references on pp.91 and 92 are to *The Powers that Be*, New York, Doubleday, 1998, pp.48, 100, 100f., 110f.

[15] *Overcoming Violence: WCC Statements*, pp.50f.

[16] An edited version of an article published in German in *Ökumenische Rundschau*, 4, 2000, pp.396ff.

[17] New York, Simon & Schuster, 1996.

[18] For the "integrated concept of culture" see Robert Schreiter, "Changing Concepts of Culture and Intercultural Theology", in Schreiter, *The New Catholicity*, Maryknoll NY, Orbis, 1997, pp.46ff.

[19] Revised and enlarged version of an article published in German in *Jahrbuch Menschenrechte 2002*, Frankfurt, Suhrkamp, 2001.

[20] These and the following references on pp.109 and 110 are to *Together on the Way*, pp.145, 195ff., 200f., 200.

[21] See UN press release SG/SM/7136 GA/9596, 20 Sept. 1999.

[22] This and the following references on pp.117 and 118 are to *Central Committee Minutes*, 2001, app. III, pp.219ff., 235, 235f., 236.

[23] This section is based on an address at the meeting of the US conference of member churches of the WCC at Atlanta, Dec. 1999, and on an article contributed to *Theology: News and Notes*, Fuller Theological Seminary, spring 2001, pp.7-10.

[24] *Central Committee Minutes*, 1999, p.92.

172

[25] This and the following references on p.124 and 125 are from "Basic Text", in *Reconciliation: Gift of God and Source of New Life*, documents from the Second European Ecumenical Assembly, Graz, June 1997, Rüdiger Noll and Stefan Vesper eds, Graz, Styria, 1998, pp.35, 37f., 39, 42, 42, 47.

[26] *Central Committee Minutes*, 1999, pp.188f.

[27] *Central Committee Minutes*, 1972, p.128.

[28] See the Kairos document, in *Challenge to the Church*, PCR Information special issue, WCC, Nov. 1985, pp.17f.

[29] Cf. Vaclav Havel, *Versuch in der Wahrheit zu leben*, Hamburg, Rowohlt, 1980.

[30] This and the following references on pp.136, 137 and 138 are from Geneviève Jacques, *Beyond Impunity*, WCC, 2000, pp.45, 45ff., 60.

III. MORAL AND SPIRITUAL FORMATION FOR A CULTURE OF LIFE

[1] *Building a World Community: Globalization and the Common Good*, Jacques Baudot ed., Copenhagen, 2000, p.45.

[2] *Ibid.*

[3] *A Global Ethic for Global Politics and Economics*, New York, Oxford. UP, 1998, p.111.

[4] *Ibid.*, pp.92f.

[5] "Costly Obedience", in *Ecclesiology and Ethics: Ecumenical Ethical Engagement, Moral Formation and the Nature of the Church*, Thomas F. Best and Martin Robra eds, WCC, 1997, p.50.

[6] "The Anguish of Man, the Praise of God and the Repentance of the Church", in *Humanum Studies 1969-75: A Collection of Documents*, WCC, 1975, p.82.

[7] "Costly Unity", p.5.

[8] "Costly Commitment", pp.39f.

[9] "Costly Obedience", pp.55f.

[10] "Costly Commitment", p.43.

[11] "Costly Unity", p.14.

[12] Cf. esp. the consultation report of 1984, *A Spirituality for Our Times*, WCC, 1985.

[13] *Signs of the Spirit*, Michael Kinnamon ed., WCC, 1991, p.112.

[14] See Cashmore and Puls, *Clearing the Way: En Route to an Ecumenical Spirituality*, WCC, 1990.

[15] Masao Takenaka, *God Is Rice: Asian Culture and Christian Faith*, WCC, 1986, pp.18f.

[16] *Ibid.*, pp.21f.

[17] See *Spirituality of the Third World*, K.C. Abraham and Bernadette Mbuy-Beya eds, Maryknoll, NY, Orbis, 1994. The references on pp.154 and 155 are from pp.3f, 197f.

[18] "Costly Obedience", pp.78f.

[19] "Working on Theology of Life", dossier, WCC Unit III Justice, Peace and Creation (n.y.), p.5.

[20] Published in *Echoes: Justice, Peace, Creation News*, 12, 1997, pp.37ff. This and the following references on pp.158 and 159 are to pp.37ff., 38f., 40.

[21] Reference is made in particular to Geiko Müller-Fahrenholz, *God's Spirit: Transforming a World in Crisis*, WCC, 1995; Larry L. Rasmussen, *Earth Community, Earth Ethics*, WCC, 1996; Lewis S. Mudge, *The Church as Moral Community: Ecclesiology and Ethics in Ecumenical Debate*, WCC, 1998. Cf. also Konrad Raiser, *Ecumenism in Transition: A Paradigm Shift in the Ecumenical Movement*, WCC, 1991.

[22] Rasmussen, *Earth Community*, p.91.

[23] *Ibid.*

[24] For a full exposition of *oikodomé* and its ecumenical significance, see Müller-Fahrenholz, *God's Spirit*, part III.

[25] Rasmussen, *Earth Community*, p.93.

[26] Müller-Fahrenholz, *God's Spirit*, pp.111f.

[27] Rasmussen, *Earth Community*, pp.171f.

[28] *Signs of the Spirit*, pp.63f.

[29] Rasmussen, *Earth Community*, p.179.

[30] This and the following references on pp.163 and 164 are to "Costly Obedience", pp.79f., 80, 81f., 87.

[31] See the report of a concluding consultation on the "Theology of Life" project at Union Theological Seminary, April 1998, in "Working on Theology of Life", p.127.

[32] Mudge, *The Church as Moral Community*, p.82.

[33] *Ibid.*, p.112.